Horace Davis

Ancestry of John Davis, governor and U. S. Senator

Horace Davis

Ancestry of John Davis, governor and U. S. Senator

ISBN/EAN: 9783337152376

Printed in Europe, USA, Canada, Australia, Japan

Cover: Foto ©Andreas Hilbeck / pixelio.de

More available books at **www.hansebooks.com**

ANCESTRY

OF

JOHN DAVIS

GOVERNOR AND U. S. SENATOR

AND

ELIZA BANCROFT

HIS WIFE

BOTH OF WORCESTER, MASSACHUSETTS

COMPILED BY HORACE DAVIS

ᵢₗ

SAN FRANCISCO, CAL.
1897

INTRODUCTION.

The following pages contain the ancestry, as far as known, of Governor John Davis and Eliza Bancroft, his wife.

Governor Davis and Mrs. Davis were both much interested in their family history, and the accounts furnished by them form the germ of this record. The work of completing it has been principally done far from the original sources of information, consequently at great disadvantage. There are some gaps in it, and many of the sketches are mere skeletons of dates, but it seemed best to finish it, imperfect as it is, rather than encounter more delay. Perhaps it may stimulate some more fortunate searcher to complete the history.

I found in the search many cases of conflicting dates, a very common difficulty in the early records. Preference has usually been given to what seemed the best authority, but sometimes I have given the reader his choice.

For greater ease in following the record, I have divided it into four groups or headings, entitled, respectively, Davis, Brigham, Bancroft, and Chandler, each being devoted to the lineage of one of the parents of Governor Davis or of his wife. The Chandler record is the most complete, as the printed sketches of the Chandler, Church, Paine, Gardiner, and Douglas families gave me the lineage of the female lines more completely than I was able to obtain in the other families. Next to this the Brigham history is fullest, where I had the aid of the Brigham and Breck printed genealogies. In following the Bancroft family, I have received much help from the manuscript notes of Mr. John M. Bancroft, and from Eaton's History of Reading. There are deficiencies in the records of the Heald and Gates families from Stow, which cannot be made up till the early history of that town becomes accessible.

The direct line of descent shows few men of wide distinction, but a very large proportion of colonial or local prominence. One man, Richard Warren, came over in the "Mayflower." Three were college graduates, two of Harvard—Robert Breck, H. C., 1700, and Aaron Bancroft, H. C., 1778, both clergymen, distinguished in their profession, —and John Davis, graduated at Yale in 1812. In the list we find two physicians—Dr. Benjamin Gott and his son-in-law, Dr. Samuel Brigham, men of standing in their day. No practicing lawyer appears on the record, except John Davis, but we have four judges presiding over county courts—Nathaniel Paine, and the second, third, and fourth John Chandlers. Only four men are rated as merchants—Francis Wainwright, Simon, his son, Stephen Paine, and Nathaniel, his son, though there may have been others. Speculators in land were plenty in the early times, but dealers in merchandise were few; the people were poor, and their wants were simple.

Military heroes are numerous, and testify to the frequency with which the Colonists were involved in wars with the French and Indians. Nearly every man was called upon some time in his life to bear arms in defence of his home, and the military title in those days usually meant actual service in the field. Among the fighting men, the most prominent were Lion Gardiner, a military engineer, who built Fort Saybrook, and held it through the Pequot troubles; Col. Benjamin Church, the most distinguished soldier of his day in the Colonial wars, and Captain Jonathan Poole, who served with distinction in the King Philip outbreak. The second, third, and fourth John Chandlers were Colonels of Worcester County Regiments, and did active service in the field. There were many others who took part in those early wars, such as Constant Southworth, Capt. Thomas Bancroft, Samuel Tarbox, Samuel Lamson, George Woodward, Capt. Samuel Bancroft, and Dr. Samuel Brigham.

In the Revolutionary War, Isaac Davis served as First Lieutenant, and Aaron Bancroft is said to have marched to Cambridge with the minute men of Reading, after Bunker Hill.

The number of men who participated in the political life of the times is remarkable. William Collier and Constant Southworth were among the leaders of Plymouth Colony in its infancy. Later, Judge Paine and the second and third John Chandlers were members of His Majesty's Council for Massachusetts Colony, and nearly half the men on our list were Deputies in the Colonial or State Legislatures; others again served as town officers, John Davis fitly closing the political record by his public service as Governor of Massachusetts, and her representative in both Houses of Congress.

Of literary material, Lion Gardiner has left us some letters and a "Relation of the Pequot Wars;" Col. Benjamin Church, his recollections of King Philip's War; Rev. Robert Breck, a few sermons; Dr. Bancroft, some sermons and a life of Washington; and Governor Davis, some political papers. A few letters from various parties are also extant, dating all the way from 1640 to 1800; but those men, as a rule, had too much use for the plough and the sword to spare time for the pen.

It will be observed that in nearly all the families which I have been able to trace to their coming over, the immigrants were of English stock, the only exception being Mary Wilemson, wife of Lion Gardiner, and all of them reached America before 1641, except the wife of David Gardiner. These conditions apply to nearly all old New England families.

To the student of heredity this record affords an interesting example of converging lines of family influence. No immigrant appears more than once; that is, no stock crosses itself; and, as a rule, a bias for some mode of life seems to run in a family. The Brecks inclined to the Church, and made much of education; the Chandlers belonged to the Colonial aristocracy, and were fond of social position; the Wainwrights leaned to mercantile pursuits; the Brecks, Wainwrights, and Bancrofts owned books, and all four of these families show many college graduates; but the great body of men in this record were farmers, for in those days the farmers comprised a very large majority of the community.

Outside of these considerations, I am well aware that nobody, except our immediate family, will take much interest in this record, and for them it has been compiled. The love of family is next to the love of country, and I would warm their hearts towards the memory of the sturdy men and women whose blood flows in their veins.

In which desire I dedicate this family history to the memory of my father and mother.

HORACE DAVIS.

San Francisco, January, 1897.

CONTENTS.

CHARTS OF DESCENT

OF

JOHN DAVIS

AND

ELIZA BANCROFT

DAVIS

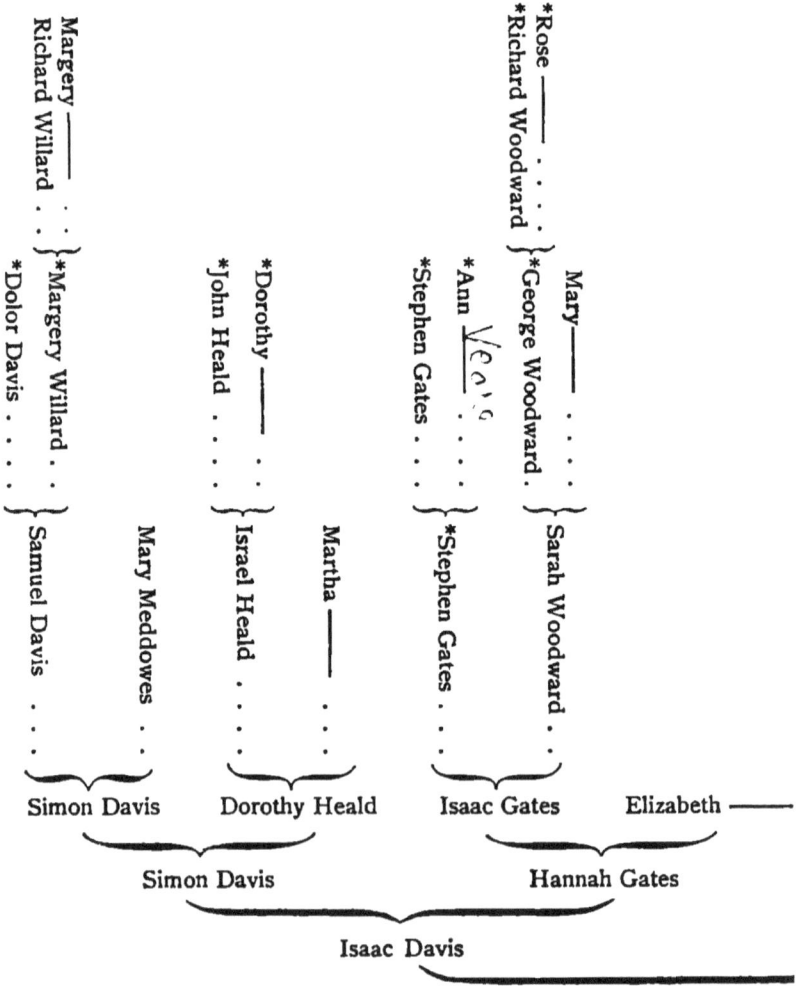

*Rose ⎫	
*Richard Woodward ⎬ *George Woodward	
Mary ⎭	Sarah Woodward
*Ann *Veare* ⎫	
*Stephen Gates ⎬ *Stephen Gates	Isaac Gates — Elizabeth
	Hannah Gates
*Dorothy ⎫	
*John Heald ⎬ Israel Heald	Dorothy Heald
Martha	Simon Davis
Margery ⎫	
Richard Willard ⎬ *Margery Willard ⎫	
*Dolor Davis ⎬ Samuel Davis	Simon Davis
Mary Meddowes	

Isaac Davis

JOHN

* Immigrants.

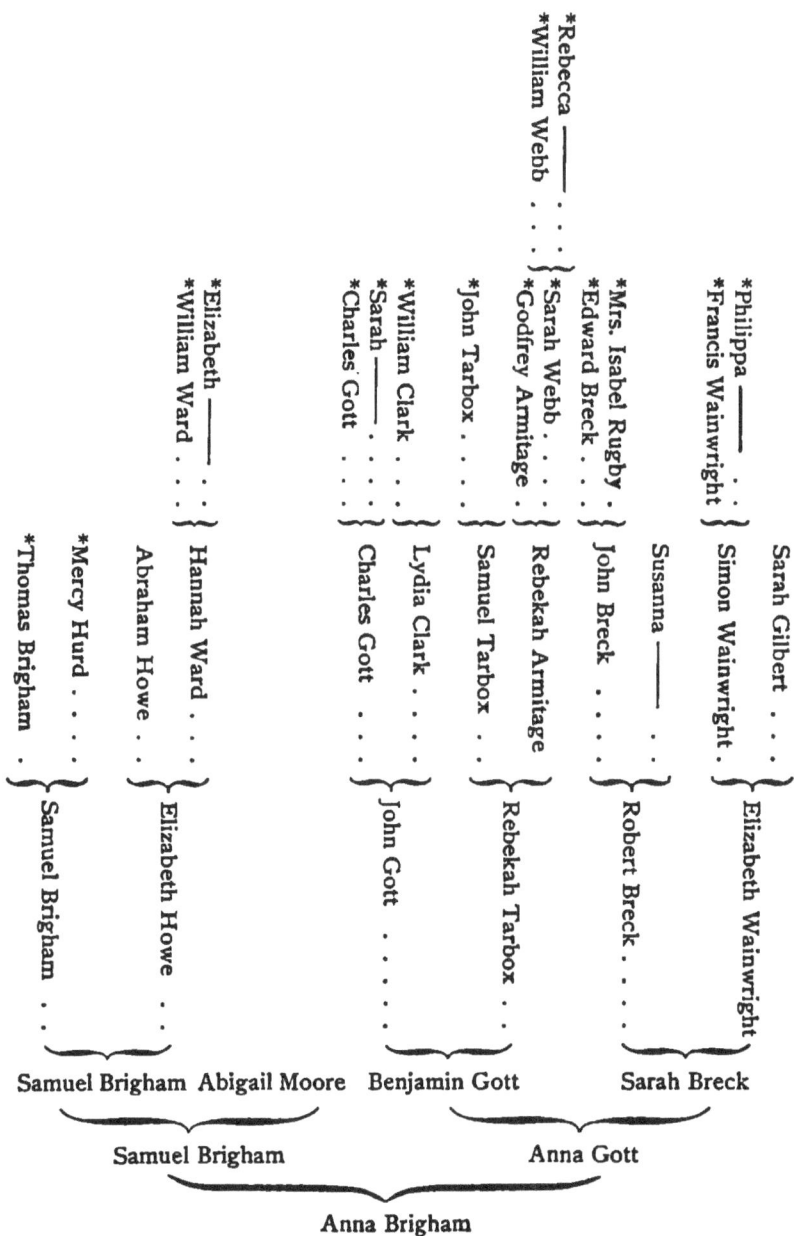

Genealogical chart (ancestors shown nested beneath each descendant):

Anna Brigham
- Samuel Brigham
  - Samuel Brigham
    - Samuel Brigham
      - *Thomas Brigham
      - *Mercy Hurd
    - Elizabeth Howe
      - Abraham Howe
      - Hannah Ward
        - *William Ward ——
        - *Elizabeth ——
  - Abigail Moore
- Anna Gott
  - Benjamin Gott
    - John Gott
      - Charles Gott
        - *Charles Gott
      - Lydia Clark
        - *William Clark
        - *Sarah
    - Rebekah Tarbox
      - Samuel Tarbox
        - John Tarbox
      - Rebekah Armitage
        - *Sarah Webb
          - *Rebecca ——
          - *William Webb
        - *Godfrey Armitage
  - Sarah Breck
    - Robert Breck
      - John Breck
        - *Mrs. Isabel Rugby
        - *Edward Breck
      - Susanna ——
    - Elizabeth Wainwright
      - Simon Wainwright
        - *Philippa ——
        - *Francis Wainwright
      - Sarah Gilbert

DAVIS

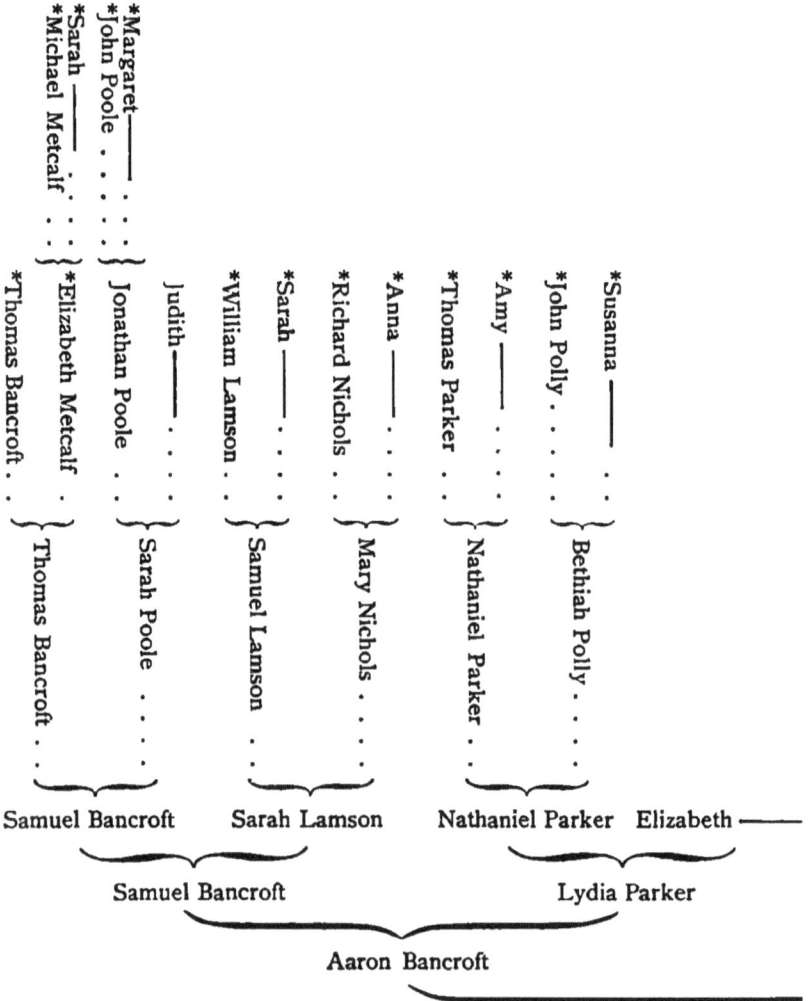

BANCROFT

*Margaret ——
*John Poole . . . . .
*Sarah ——
*Michael Metcalf . . . .

*Thomas Bancroft . . .
*Elizabeth Metcalf .
Jonathan Poole .
Judith ——
*William Lamson .
*Sarah ——
*Richard Nichols .
*Anna ——
*Thomas Parker . .
*Amy ——
*John Polly . . . . .
*Susanna ——

Thomas Bancroft .
*Elizabeth Metcalf .
Sarah Poole . .
Judith ——
Samuel Lamson .
Mary Nichols . . . .
Nathaniel Parker . .
Bethiah Polly . . . . .

Samuel Bancroft   Sarah Lamson   Nathaniel Parker   Elizabeth ——

Samuel Bancroft   Lydia Parker

Aaron Bancroft

ELIZA

CHANDLER

Generation (earliest, single names at far left):

- Thomas Mattle . . .
- Dericke Wilemson .
- Hochim Bastians .
- Alexander Carpenter

First named generation:

- *William Chandler
- *Annis Alcock .
- *William Douglas .
- *Ann Mattle . .
- *Richard Raymond .
- *Judith ——— .
- *Nehemiah Smith .
- *Sarah ——— .
- *Lion Gardiner .
- *Mary Wilemson .
- *William King .
- *Dorothy Hayne .
- *William Ludlam .
- *Clemence ———
- *Richard Warren .
- *Mrs. Elizabeth Marsh
- Edward Southworth
- *Alice Carpenter
- *William Collier .
- *Stephen Paine .
- *Rose ——— .
- *Edward Rainsford .
- *John Sunderland .
- *Dorothy ———

Next generation:

- *John Chandler . . .
- Elizabeth Douglas .
- Joshua Raymond .
- Elizabeth Smith . .
- David Gardiner .
- *Mrs. Mary Leringham
- *Samuel King . .
- Abigail Ludlam . .
- *Richard Church .
- *Elizabeth Warren .
- *Constant Southworth
- *Elizabeth Collier . .
- *Nathaniel Paine . .
- Elizabeth ——— .
- Jonathan Rainsford .

Next generation:

- John Chandler
- Mary Raymond .
- John Gardiner .
- Mary King . . . . .
- Benjamin Church .
- Alice Southworth .
- Nathaniel Paine . .
- Mary Sunderland .
- Dorothy Rainsford .

Next generation (four lines):

- John Chandler
- Hannah Gardiner
- Charles Church
- Hannah Paine

Next generation:

- John Chandler
- Mary Church

Descendant:

- Lucretia Chandler

BANCROFT

BOOK PLATE.

(Suggested by incident recorded on page 21.)

DAVIS.

Dolor.
Samuel.
Simon.
Simon.
Isaac.
John.

DOLOR DAVIS, Cambridge, 1634. Immigrant. Born about 1593, according to Amos Otis. The first positive knowledge we have of him is contained in the will of Edward Clarke, gent., of East Fairleigh, County Kent, England, made 13 July, 1614, proved 1 November, 1614, containing this clause: "I give to my servant Dolor Davis my house and lands in the parish of Marden."

Ten years later, on 29 March, 1624, Dolor Davis and Margery Willard were married at East Fairleigh. She was daughter of Richard Willard, yeoman, of Horsemonden, County Kent, by his second wife, Margery, and was christened 7 November, 1602. Margery's mother was buried 12 December, 1608; Willard died in February, 1617, and his widow, Margery's step-mother, Joan, followed him soon after. By his will, he left considerable property, mainly in lands, part of which came to Margery. Simon Willard, her brother, sailed with his family for New England, in May, 1634, and probably Davis came in the same vessel, leaving his family behind him.

On 4 August, 1634, Davis and Willard were granted lands in Cambridge, Mass. On 17 April, 1635, "Margaret Davies," with three small children, sailed from London for New England, in the "Elizabeth." On 4 June, 1635, Davis was granted house lot in Cambridge.

In August, 1635, he sold his lands, and probably moved to Duxbury, where we find him in 1638–39, and where he received two grants of land in 1640. The same year he took part in founding Barnstable, though he did not move there until 1643.

In 1641, he went on the bond of George Willard, his brother-in-law, signing as a "Planter of Scituate."

On 1 March, 1641–2, on a jury at Plymouth.

In 1643, on list of inhabitants of Barnstable able to bear arms.

On 4 June, 1645, member of Grand Inquest of Plymouth Colony.

On 2 June, 1646, admitted freeman.

On 27 August, 1648, dismissed from Duxbury Church to Barnstable Church.

On 3 June, 1652, chosen Surveyor of Highways.

On 6 June, 1654, chosen Constable.

In 1655, removed to Concord, Mass.

William Martin and others having petitioned the General Court of Massachusetts Colony for a grant of land in what is now Groton, Mass., Davis and seven others, on the 25 May, 1655, were appointed Selectmen of this new settlement, and in 1656 his name appears on a petition for remission of taxes in Groton; but he seems never to have made Groton his home, for on 20 August, 1655, he bought of Roger Draper his farm and house in Concord. In the conveyance he is called "a husbandman."

Meantime he sold his Barnstable property for "corn and cattle," the documents recording the various payments, and the transfer itself, being in the Plymouth records. In them he is styled a "house-carpenter." Margery Davis joins in the acknowledgment, which is the last record of her. She probably died at Concord, between 1658 and 1667.

In 1659, lands were granted him in Concord; and in 1664 he signed a petition to the General Court as an inhabitant of Concord.

Of the three children brought over from England, John and Mary were married and settled on the Cape. Elizabeth probably died young. Three more children were born in America; and they, too, were married and settled, but near or in Concord.

In 1666, Davis left Concord and returned to Barnstable, and

was again admitted as an inhabitant there, where his name appears on various documents.

He married, probably in 1671, Mrs. Joanna Bursley, widow of Capt. John Bursley, and daughter of Rev. Joseph Hull. On 13 September, 1672, he made his will, which was proved 2 July, 1673; inventory taken 19 June, 1673. He probably died early in June, 1673, at the ripe old age, says Amos Otis, of eighty years.

His widow, Joanna, was living in 1683. His will recites that he had provided for his sons Simon and Samuel, and then he bequeaths his house and land in Concord, in all one hundred and three acres, to his son John, adding: "I also bequeath to him my carpenter's tools and my serge suit and cloke." His personal property goes mainly to his widow and daughters. He mentions his "dwelling-house in Barnstable," but disposes of no real estate there; perhaps it belonged to his son John, who afterwards occupied it. The widow, probably, had property in her own right, derived from Capt. Bursley. The inventory of Davis's real estate and personal property in Concord was appraised at £125 5s. 7d.

Children—all by wife, Margery:

1. John, born in England about 1626.
2. Mary, born in England about 1631.
3. Elizabeth, born in England about 1633.
4. Simon, born in America about 1636.
5. SAMUEL, born in America about 1639–40.
6. Ruth, born in America; baptized 24 March, 1644–5.

SAMUEL DAVIS, of Concord, Mass., son of Dolor. Born about 1639 or 1640. Married at Lynn, 11 January, 1665–6, Mary Meddowes, parentage unknown; seven children. Lived in Concord, and styled himself in deeds "husbandman" and "yeoman."

On 20 November, 1680, Samuel Davis and Mary, his wife, of Groton, conveyed to Justinian Holden, of Groton, twenty acres of land; consideration, fifteen pounds "current money." Probably this was part of his father's purchase in Groton in 1655. If Samuel Davis ever lived in Groton, it must have been for a very short time, as the births of all his children appear on the Concord records.

Freeman, 21 March, 1689–90.

In 1696, he purchased two parcels of land in the east part of Concord, as follows: 12 April, of Thomas Wheeler, four acres for forty shillings; and 10 November, of John Jones and others twenty acres for eight pounds; also, 17 December, 1705, of Samuel Fox, six acres for six pounds. In all these instruments he is styled Samuel Davis, Senior, husbandman.

I suppose these were parts of his homestead in what is now the west part of Bedford. The property is still in possession of his descendants; the present house, which is now one hundred and fifty years old, being erected on the site of Samuel Davis's homestead.

On 2 June, 1696, he petitioned Concord authorities for a bridle-path to his house from Billerica Road.

In 1698 and 9, Samuel Davis, Senior, chosen Fence-viewer for east part of Concord.

In 1706, he conveyed houses and land to his two "well-beloved sons" "in consideration of good will and affection," viz: to Eleazer his dwelling and thirty-nine acres, and to Daniel his dwelling and fifty-one acres. Here he called himself "yeoman," and his sons "husbandmen." His wife Mary joined in the conveyances, and both made their "marks."

Mary, his wife, died 3 October, 1710, and on 18 October, 1711, he married second wife, Ruth Taylor.

On 8 May, 1712, he sold to Eleazer Davis, a house, barn, and nine acres of land for fifty pounds. He himself signed his autograph signature; his wife Ruth made her "mark."

On 6 August, 1720, wife Ruth died.

Samuel Davis distributed most of his real estate to his sons during his life, and died after 1720; date of death and place of burial unknown.

Children—all by wife, Mary:

1. Mercy, born 27 October, 1666; died young.
2. Samuel, born 21 June, 1669.
3. Daniel, born 16 or 26 March, 1673.
4. Mary, born 12 August, 1677.
5. Eleazer, born 26 July, 1680.
6. SIMON, born 9 August, 1683.
7. Stephen, born 30 March, 1686.

Lieut. SIMON DAVIS (Senior), of Holden, son of Samuel. Born 9 August, 1683, at Concord, Mass. Married in 1713, Dorothy, daughter of Israel Heald, of Stow. She was born about 1692. Eight children; three born in Concord, five probably in Rutland. He began life in Concord; but about 1720 removed to Rutland, Mass., among the first settlers. Tradition says he was obliged to carry his plow on his back for some miles, for want of roads. 10 June, 1720, signed petition to proprietors for division of meadow-land in Rutland.

On 30 September, 1720, chosen one of the committee of three to cover and enclose meeting-house.

In July, 1722, chosen Selectman.

In 1723, waylaid by Indians; narrow escape from death.

On 9 October, 1727, at organization of first church, signed "Solemn Covenant" with Rev. Mr. Frink and others; then chosen, with Capt. Samuel Knight and others, to sign letters inviting Council of Pastors and Delegates to establish church.

On 1 November, 1727, Rev. Robert Breck, of Marlboro, being Moderator of Council to ordain Rev. Mr. Frink, Simon Davis produced letters of dismissal from Concord Church to Rutland Church.

Soon after sold his lands in Rutland, and settled in the northern part of Worcester.

On 13 August, 1734, records of Court of General Sessions at Worcester show that "Lieut. Davis" was licensed as tavern-keeper and retailer in the township of Worcester.

On 10 March, 1735, John Chandler, Henry Lee, Esq.,

Simon Davis, and seven others, chosen surveyors of highways at Worcester.

On 12 August, 1735, again licensed as tavern-keeper, and went on tavern-keeper's bond of Caleb Wetherbee, of Southboro. Same year, at November term of Court, sat on jury in two cases of men convicted of " neglecting the Lord's Day."

On 1 March, 1735–6, same persons as above again chosen surveyors of highways.

On 2 May, 1737, chosen to same office for northern half of Worcester.

On 13 May, 1740, with others, petitioned General Court to be set off in a separate township.

On 4 May, 1741, Moderator of first town meeting in Holden; also chosen Chairman of Selectmen, and grand jury man.

In 1741–43, Selectman.

In 1742, Assessor.

He died 16 February, 1763, in his eightieth year; wife Dorothy died 21 July, 1776, in her eighty-fourth year. Their gravestones are standing in Holden; on both he is styled " Lieut. Simon Davis."

Children:

1. SIMON, born at Concord, 17 May, 1714.
2. Israel, born at Concord, 31 August, 1717.
3. Joseph, born at Concord, 16 July, 1720; H. C. 1740.
4. Elizur.
5. Oliver.
6. Dolly.
7. Martha.
8. Azubah.

SIMON DAVIS (2d), of Rutland, son of Simon (1st). Born in Concord, 17 May, 1714. His parents moved to Rutland about 1720. Married, about 1733, Hannah, daughter of Ensign Isaac Gates, of Stow. She was born at Stow, 2 April, 1714.

Davis lived in Rutland, "at the foot of the hill near the tan-

ISAAC DAVIS.

ISAAC DAVIS'S HOUSE NORTHBORO, MASS., 1775 TO 1850.

yard," and was a farmer. I have no record of his taking any part in public affairs. He had a family of eleven children. He died suddenly, 9 April, 1754, not quite forty years old. The house of a friend named Smith, in Holden, had burned down, and the neighbors assembled to help him rebuild. As Davis was sawing off a timber, he said, "My head feels strange," and fell dead.

His wife Hannah, six years later, contracted the smallpox by nursing a sick friend, and died 7 January, 1761, in her forty-seventh year. She was buried in a pasture on the farm, but several years later her son David removed her body in the night and buried it beside her husband. Their gravestones are standing in the old churchyard on the hill in Rutland.

Davis died intestate; his estate was appraised in 1754 at £445 0s. 7d., but was not distributed till 1763, after his widow's death. The order for the inventory is signed by John Chandler, Justice of Peace, and the order for distribution by John Chandler, Judge of Probate.

Children:

1. Elizabeth, born January, 1735; died young.
2. Hannah, born March, 1736.
3. Miriam, born June, 1738.
4. David, born January, 1740.
5. Elizabeth, born 19 June, 1742.
6. Simon, born 17 April, 1744; died young.
7. Mercy, born 6 June, 1745.
8. Simon, born August, 1747.
9. Isaac, born 27 February, 1749.
10. Samuel, born 15 February, 1751.
11. John, born 13 September, 1752.

Deacon Isaac Davis, of Northboro; son of Simon, of Rutland. Born in Rutland, 27 February, 1749. Losing both parents in childhood, he was brought up by his sister, Mrs. Miriam Fairbanks, of Sterling; and, later, went to live with his elder brother, David, in Paxton, to learn the trade of a tanner.

About 1770, he went to Westboro, to construct a tanyard for Capt. Maynard, and instruct his son in the business.   There he met and married, 21 May, 1772, Anna Brigham, stepdaughter of Maynard, and daughter of Dr. Samuel Brigham, deceased. She was born on 29 October, 1753.

They settled in Westboro, between the Maynard house and the Assabet River, where four children were born.

On the breaking out of the Revolutionary War, he enlisted in the Massachusetts militia, and on 10 June, 1779, was commissioned First Lieutenant Third Company (Capt. James Godfrey) of the Sixth Worcester County Regiment, Col. Cushing commanding.   On 3 July, 1780, he paid his brother-in-law, Dr. Samuel Brigham, four hundred pounds to "do duty for him in the service for the term of three months."   Brigham acted as paymaster, and was present at the capture of Smith, Andre's guide.

In 1781, Davis purchased of the Widow Elizabeth Gray, of Boston, the house and farm just across the river in Northboro, where he lived the rest of his life.   There he built a tanyard, and pursued that business till his eldest two sons became of age, when he turned over the tanyard to them, and devoted himself to his farm.   Six more children were born to them in Northboro. On 24 April, 1803, his wife Anna died.

He married his second wife in December, 1804,— Mrs. Susanna (Baker) Harrington; she died on 11 January, 1816; no children.

He married his third wife on 3 October, 1816,— Mrs. Elizabeth (Baker) Thurston, sister of his second wife; no children.

Isaac Davis was a man of strong character and public spirit, taking a lively interest in public affairs.   On 7 August, 1786, he was chosen delegate to a County Convention held at Leicester on 15 August.   Among other things, he was instructed to vote to petition the General Court to do away with lawyers.

He represented Northboro in the General Court twelve years (1787–1798), and was Deacon of the First Church thirty years (1795–1825).   He is sometimes called "Lieutenant."

He died on 27 April, 1826; buried in Northboro.

His widow Elizabeth died on 29 March, 1850.

Children—all by wife, Anna:

1. Phineas, born 12 September, 1772.
2. Joseph, born 28 February, 1774.
3. Anna, born 19 June, 1777.
4. Isaac, born 23 September, 1779.
5. Sarah Breck, born 6 August, 1782.
6. Samuel, born 22 January, 1784.
7. JOHN, born 13 January, 1787; Yale, 1812.
8. Hannah, born 10 December, 1789.
9. Eliza, born 15 October, 1794.
10. Rebecca, born 8 July, 1796.

Gov. JOHN DAVIS, of Worcester, son of Isaac, of Northboro. Born in Northboro, 13 January, 1787. Graduated at Yale, in 1812. Studied law with Hon. Francis Blake; admitted to bar in 1815; and established himself at Spencer.

In May, 1816, removed to Worcester, and became partner in law business with Levi Lincoln, later with Charles Allen, later with Emory Washburn. On 28 March, 1822, married Eliza, daughter of Rev. Aaron Bancroft, of Worcester; she was born on 17 February, 1791.

In 1823, member of Board of School Overseers; 1824, chosen Representative to United States Congress; re-elected Congressman four times.

In 1831, President Worcester Agricultural Society.

In 1833, elected Governor of Massachusetts.

In 1834, re-elected Governor of Massachusetts.

In 1834, President of Worcester Lyceum.

In 1835, chosen United States Senator.

In 1840, elected Governor third time.

In 1841, elected Governor fourth time.

In 1842, nominated, but defeated.

In 1845, again chosen United States Senator.

In 1847, elected Senator third time.

In 1853, retired to private life; resumed law.

On 19 April, 1854, died at Worcester.

Gov. Davis held other honorable positions; but as his life is part of the history of the State and Nation, I have thought it unnecessary to give more than a mere skeleton of his career.

Mrs. Davis died at Worcester, on 24 January, 1872. She was a woman of bright, cheerful disposition, coupled with unusual vigor and activity. Although pressed by the cares of a large household, she managed to keep in touch with the thought and literature of her day, and found time to bear her part in all public matters needing the help of women. She spent several winters at Washington, where she was long remembered for her delightful companionship. To the end of her long life she enjoyed the society of young people, who were drawn to her by the freshness of youth tempered by the wisdom of years.

Children:

1. John Chandler Bancroft; H. C., 1840; LL. D., Columbia; Assistant Secretary of State; Minister Plenipotentiary to Germany; Judge Court of Claims.
2. George Henry.
3. Bruyn Hasbrouck; Williams, 1845; Brigadier-General in Civil War.
4. Horace; H. C., 1849: LL.D., University of the Pacific; Member of Congress; President University of California.
5. Andrew McFarland; S. B., Harvard College, 1854, and A. M., 1893.

HEALD.

John Heald, of Concord. Immigrant. Came, by tradition, from Berwick on Tweed. Freeman, 2 June, 1641.

Wife, Dorothy; four sons and four daughters. Some, perhaps, born in England.

John Heald (Senior) died on 24 May, 1662. Will names only three eldest children — John, Timothy, Hannah — as having received their shares.

Children:
John.
Timothy.
Hannah.
Dorcas, born 22 May, 1645; died 1 May, 1650.
Gershom, born 23 March, 1647.
Dorothy, born 16 October, 1649.
ISRAEL, born 1660.
And perhaps others.

ISRAEL HEALD of Stow, probably son of John, of Concord. Born about 1660; in 1683 owned land in Stow with his brother, Gershom. Married Martha ———; parentage unknown. He lived in Stow and was a blacksmith. He died 7 September, 1738, aged 78; his will is on record in East Cambridge, and mentions sons, Oliver and Benjamin, and daughter, Dorothy; also grandson, Joseph Davis, son of Dorothy, and adds, "as for my other children, I hope and advise them to be content with what I have given them."

Widow Martha died 14 June, 1746. Both are buried at Stow.
This Joseph Davis was the Holden minister, H. C., 1740.

Children:
DOROTHY, married Lieut. Simon Davis.
Israel.
Oliver.
Benjamin, and other children.

GATES.

Stephen.
Stephen.
Isaac.
Hannah, married Simon Davis, of Rutland.

STEPHEN GATES, of Hingham, 1638. Immigrant. The accounts of the earlier part of his life are conflicting. He is said to have been second son of Thomas Gates, of Norwich,

Eng. Married in England, wife, Ann, parentage unknown; came over in the "Diligent," in 1638, with wife, two sons, and one daughter; was at Hingham, in 1638. Inventory of estate of Capt. Bozone Allen, 22 September, 1652, (Suffolk Wills) shows Stephen Gates, of Hingham, among debtors. Gates removed to Cambridge; thence, in 1653, to "Nashaway" (Lancaster), where he signed, in 1654, petition for incorporation. Freeman, in 1656; constable at Nashaway, in 1657; returned to Cambridge, where he hired a farm, as shown by his will, made on 9 June, 1662, and proved on 7 October, 1662. In his will he calls himself of Cambridge. Widow Ann, married second husband, in 1663, Richard Woodward, of Watertown, and died in Stow, on 5 February, 1683.

Children:

Elizabeth, born in England; married, November, 1649, John Lazell.

STEPHEN, married, about 1664, Sarah Woodward.

Simon, born in America.

Mary, married, 5 April, 1658, John Maynard.

Thomas.

STEPHEN GATES, Junior, of Boston, son of Stephen, was born in England; came over with his parents; married, about 1664, Sarah, daughter of George Woodward, of Watertown. She was born on 6 February, 1642–3.

He was living in Boston in 1667; lived also in Cambridge and Charlestown. In 1673, he purchased of Edward Drinker, of Boston, 300 acres of land on Assabet River, in Stow.

Removed to Marlboro about 1678, where his youngest three children were born.

His will, dated at Stow, 5 September, 1701, was probated on 15 September, 1707.

Children:

1. Stephen, born 17 July, 1665.
2. Simon, born 5 March, 1666–7, at Cambridge.
3. Thomas, born in 1669.

4. ISAAC, born in 1673.
5. Nathaniel.

The next three were born in Marlboro:

6. Sarah, born in 1679.
7. Rebecca, born in 1682.
8. Daniel, born in 1685.

ISAAC GATES, Ensign, son of Stephen, Jr.; born in 1673. Wife, Elizabeth; parentage unknown. He died at Stow, on 22 November, 1748, aged seventy-five.

Child:

HANNAH, born at Stow, 2 April, 1714. Married Simon Davis.
Perhaps other children.

I hope to be able to trace this family further.

WOODWARD.

Richard.
George.
Sarah, married Stephen Gates.

RICHARD WOODWARD, of Watertown. Immigrant. Came in the "Elizabeth," from Ipswich, 10 October, 1634, aged forty-five, with wife Rose, aged fifty, and two children—George and John,—each stated to be thirteen years old. Freeman, 2 September, 1635.

Wife Rose died on 6 August (or October), 1662.

He married, 18 April, 1663, Ann, widow of Stephen Gates, of Cambridge, after which he lived in Cambridge. Woodward died 16 February, 1664-5.

Widow Ann died 5 February, 1682-3, at Stow.

Children—by wife, Rose—both born in England:

GEORGE.
John.

GEORGE WOODWARD, Watertown, 1641, son of Richard. Born in England about 1619. Came over with his parents, 1634. First wife, Mary ———; parentage unknown, eight children. Freeman, 6 May, 1646; married, 17 August, 1659, second wife, Elizabeth, daughter of Thomas Hammond, of Cambridge (Newton). In the list of soldiers in King Philip's War, Watertown is credited with £0. 7s. 8d. on George Woodward's account, probably money advanced his family during his absence on service.

Woodward died 31 May, 1676. Widow Elizabeth married second husband, Samuel Truesdale, his second wife.

Children—by first wife, Mary:

1. Amos, born about 1640; died 9 October, 1679; aged thirty-eight.
2. Mary, born 12 August, 1641.
3. SARAH, born 3 (or 6) February, 1642–3; married Stephen Gates, of Boston.
4. Rebecca, born 30 December, 1647.
5. John, born 20 (or 28) March, 1649; married second wife, Sarah, daughter of Thos. Bancroft.
6. Susanna, born 30 September, 1651.
7. Daniel, born 2 September, 1653.
8. Mercy, born 3 June, 1656.

By second wife, Elizabeth:

9. George, born 11 September, 1660.
10. Thomas, born 15 September, 1662; died 3 September, 1666.
11. Elizabeth, born 8 May, 1664.
12. Nathaniel, born 28 May, 1668; died 28 May, 1668.
13. Sarah, born 3 October, 1675.

BRIGHAM.

Thomas.
Samuel.
Samuel.
Samuel.
Anna, married Isaac Davis.

THOMAS BRIGHAM, of Cambridge. Immigrant. Born in England, about 1603; came to America in 1635, in the "Susan and Ellen," as "a servant, age thirty-two." Member of Cambridge Church before 1637; freeman, 18 April, 1637; lived in 1638 on easterly corner Brattle and Ash Streets, Cambridge.

Married, before 1642, Mercy Hurd, parentage unknown. Settled on north side Charles River, on the line between Cambridge and Watertown; built house there. Constable, 1639–42; Selectman, 1639–40, '42, and '47. Accumulated considerable property; afterwards, about 1648, bought land and built house in what is now Somerville. He had two bound "servants," five horses, fourteen sheep, and ten cattle.

In 1652, had 180 acres of land allotted to him in Shawshine (now Billerica). He made his will 17 January, 1653–4, signed with his mark, and died the next day, aged about fifty; will proved 3 October, 1654. The inventory footed up £449. 4s. 9d.

Widow Mercy married at Sudbury, 1 March, 1655, her second husband, — Edmund Rice, of Sudbury, by whom she had two daughters; on her second marriage she took with her to Sudbury her Brigham children, all young. Rice died in 1663, and she married in 1664 her third husband, —William Hunt, — and moved to Marlboro, where Hunt died in 1667. Mrs. Mercy Hunt died 23 December, 1693.

I have before me a letter of Rev. Edmund Browne, of Sudbury, 27 November, 1666, stating that Mrs. Hunt had been regularly transferred from the Cambridge Church to Sudbury

Church, and, as she was about to leave Sudbury, he recommends her to other churches.

I have also a vigorous protest, apparently in her own hand-writing, addressed to "the Honoured Committee of Marlborough," 4 July, 1673, defending her meadow rights. William Hunt's original will, made 6 July, 1667, is also in my possession.

Children :

1. Thomas, born about 1642.
2. John, born 9 March, 1644–5.
3. Mary.
4. Hannah, born 9 March, 1650–1.
5. SAMUEL, born 12 January, 1652–3.

Capt. SAMUEL BRIGHAM, of Marlboro; son of Thomas. Born 12 January, 1652–3, at Cambridge. When his mother married William Hunt, she probably took her Brigham children to her new home in Marlboro, for in 1681 the sons join in several conveyances of land belonging to the father's estate in Watertown and Cambridge, styling themselves "all of Marlboro." On 1 October, 1675, in King Philip's War, Brigham was assigned to defend the house of Abraham Williams.

About 1684, he married Elizabeth Howe, probably daughter of Abraham Howe, of Watertown; she was born 5 April, 1665.

In 1686, with others, he purchased of the Indians, 6000 acres near Marlboro. In 1688, under Andros, Samuel Brigham was taxed for person and estate, £0. 4s. 3d.

In 1690, admitted freeman.

Representative, 1697–99, 1705.

Town Treasurer, 1699–1703.

Selectman, 1707, 1710.

His name appears on the records repeatedly in business transactions. In 1694, he sold land to Beman. In 1695, July 28, with his brothers, he brought suit against Fessenden about matters connected with his father's estate; in 1707, drew twenty-one acres in division of land; and in 1708, purchased ten and a-half acres of Obadiah Ward.

He was a tanner and farmer, and his tan-yard is occupied by his descendants still. "He lived a mile and a quarter east of the Academy in Marlboro," and died intestate, 24 July, 1713, aged sixty, leaving several young children. Estate distributed 12 March, 1719–20; valued at £2190 in Province bills. I have original inventory. Widow Elizabeth died 26 July, 1735, in her seventy-fifth year. Their gravestones are standing in Marlboro. Brigham's gravestone says he died "in the fifty-ninth year of his age," which is probably incorrect.

Children:

1. Elizabeth, born 24 March, 1685.
2. Hepsibah, born 25 January, 1686.
3. SAMUEL, born 25 January, 1689.
4. Lydia, born 6 March, 1691.
5. Jedediah, born 8 June, 1693.
6. Jotham, born 23 December, 1695.
7. Timothy, born 10 October, 1698.
8. Charles, born 30 December, 1700.
9. Persis, born 10 July, 1703.
10. Antipas, born 16 October, 1706.

Esquire SAMUEL BRIGHAM (2d), of Marlboro; often styled Captain; son of Samuel (1st). Born 25 January, 1689; married, 23 August, 1716, Abigail Moore, parentage unknown. She was born about 1696.

He settled in the south part of Marlboro, and was a leading man for many years.

In 1716, he was on the committee "to seat the meeting." In December, 1727, one of a company to whom leave was granted by General Court to purchase of the Indians what is now Grafton.

Brigham was often moderator of town meetings; was Assessor 1739–40; Town Treasurer; Selectman, 1741, '42, '44, '46, '48, '49; Representative, 1741; that year on the tax list of Marlboro he had two polls, two houses, two acres orchard, forty acres mowing, forty acres pasture, nine acres tillage, twelve oxen, ten cows, three horses, forty sheep and goats, and three swine.

Wife Abigail died 20 November, 1731, aged 35, leaving a large family of young children. Brigham survived her many years; in 1747–49, he administered on the estate of his brother Antipas. I find no record of his death.

Children:

1. Samuel, born 13 June, 1717, died young.
2. Sybilla, born 15 October, 1718.
3. Mary, born 13 April, 1720.
4. Abigail, born 10 December, 1721.
5. SAMUEL, born 3 March, 1723–4.
6. Phineas, born 18 December, 1725.
7. Uriah, born 10 September, 1727.
8. George, born 17 March, 1730.

Dr. SAMUEL BRIGHAM (3d), of Marlboro; son of Esquire Samuel (2d). Born 3 March, 1723–4; married first wife 24 November, 1747, Elizabeth Wood, who died without offspring. " He was a physician," says my father, " of considerable eminence. He visited Europe, partly for his health and partly for study in his profession." He seems to have traveled considerably for those times; was at Kingston, Jamaica, 21 April, 1748. On 9 January, 1752, he married second wife, Anna, daughter of Dr. Benjamin Gott, of Marlboro. She was born 8 January, 1731. Dr. Brigham was in the army, October, 1755, at Crown Point, probably as surgeon.

Dr. Samuel Chandler's diary of his trip to Crown Point, 2 October, 1755, as Chaplain of a Massachusetts regiment, says, "Our Company now is Dr. Brigham, Dr. Got," and others. I have seen an original letter from Dr. Brigham to his father, dated at Crown Point.

He was Town Clerk of Marlboro; Selectman in 1754–5, and died suddenly 22 February, 1756, aged thirty-three years.

Widow Anna married second husband, Capt. Maynard, of Westboro, and died 6 July, 1799, in her sixty-ninth year; gravestone in Westboro.

Children—all by wife, Anna:

1. Elizabeth, born 11 August, 1752.
2. ANNA, born 29 October, 1753; married Isaac Davis.
3. Susanna, born 12 April, 1755.
4. Samuel, born 21 August, 1756, posthumous child; A. B. Dartmouth, 1779; A. M. and M. D. He was my grandfather's substitute in the Revolutionary Army, serving as Paymaster; and was present at the capture of Smith, Andre's guide.

HOWE.

Abraham.
Elizabeth, married Samuel Brigham (1st).

ABRAHAM HOWE, of Watertown. Born probably about 1635; married 6 March, 1657, (Ward), [6 May, 1657, (Hudson), 26 March, 1658, (Savage)], Hannah Ward, daughter of William Ward, of Sudbury; she was born in 1639. He removed, in 1660, to Marlboro, where he kept an inn, and died 30 June, 1695, (30 January, 1695, Ward).

Widow Hannah, made will 1 June, 1716, and died 3 November, 1717, aged seventy-eight.

Children (Hudson):

1. Daniel, born 1658.
2. Mary, born 1659, in Watertown.
3. Joseph, born 1661.

Born in Marlboro:

4. Hannah, born 9 November, 1663.
5. ELIZABETH, born 5 April, 1665; married Samuel Brigham.
6. Deborah, born 1 March, 1667.
7. Rebecca, born 4 February, 1668.
8. Abraham, born 8 October, 1670.
9. Sarah, born 20 December, 1672.
10. Abigail, born 4 March, 1675.

This Abraham Howe has generally been considered to be the son of Abraham Howe, of Roxbury; immigrant; freeman, 2 May, 1638, who died 20 November, 1683, leaving six children or more. But Mr. Savage disputes it.

WARD.

William.
Hannah, married Abraham Howe.

Deacon WILLIAM WARD, of Sudbury, 1639. Immigrant. Born about 1600. His deposition, taken in 1644, gives his age as forty-four, or thereabouts. Ward came over, in 1639, with five children; owned lands in Sudbury, 1639; married, about 1639, second wife, Elizabeth, parentage unknown.

On 10 May, 1643, freeman.

In 1644, represented Sudbury in General Court.

Chairman of Selectmen in Sudbury for several years; eight children born there. In 1656, petitioned General Court for the plantation of Marlboro. Removed in 1660 to Marlboro; represented it in General Court in 1666; deacon at first organization of church.

In King Philip's War, 1675, three soldiers were assigned to defend "Deacon Ward's House," and he signed his assent to the distribution of arms. It is stated in the "Ward Family" that "his buildings were fired, his cattle destroyed, and one of his sons slain." Ward made his will 6 April, 1686, and died 10 August, 1687. Widow Elizabeth appears on tax list under Andros, 1688; her rate was £o. os. 11d. She died, 9 December, 1700, aged eighty-six or eighty-seven; grave-stone in Marlboro.

Children—by first wife—all born in England:

1. John, born about 1626.
2. Joanna, born about 1628.
3. Obadiah, born about 1632.
4. Richard, born about 1635.
5. Deborah, born about 1637.

By second wife, Elizabeth—born in America:

6. HANNAH, born 1639; married Abraham Howe.
7. William, born 22 January, 1640.
8. Samuel, born 24 September, 1641.
9. Elizabeth, born 14 April, 1643.
10. Increase, born 22 February, 1645.
11. Hopestill, born 24 February, 1646.
12. Mary, born about 1647.
13. Eleazer, born about 1649.
14. Bethia, born about 1658.

GOTT.

Charles.
Charles.
John.
Benjamin.
Anna, married Samuel Brigham.

Deacon CHARLES GOTT, of Salem. Immigrant. Came in the "Abigail" with Endicott, September, 1628. In 1629, wrote Gov. Bradford a letter about the election of Skelton as pastor.

On 19 October, 1630, requested admission as freeman; admitted 18 May, 1631; first deacon of church.

Wife, Sarah, parentage unknown; three children.

In 1635, Representative.

In 1641, Deacon Gott received instruction from Rev. Hugh Peters on his departure for England relative to his property. On 3 March, 1653, Peters wrote from London to Gott at Wenham.

In 1653, bought of John Killiam, of Wenham, dwelling-house and lands, and moved from Salem to Wenham, where he was on first Board of Selectmen.

From 1654 to 1666, Representative from Wenham.

In 1659, paid £3 in corn for minister.

On 8 December, 1663, Gott and wife admitted to Wenham Church.

In 1665, wife, Sarah, died. He died 15 January, 1667–8.

Children:

1. Deborah, baptized 12 February, 1636–7.
2. CHARLES, baptized June, 1639.
3. Daniel, baptized 28 June, 1646.

Lieut. CHARLES GOTT, of Wenham; son of Charles. Baptized June, 1639. Married 12 November, 1659, Sarah Dennis, possibly daughter of Edward Dennis, of Boston, 1636.

On 8 December, 1663, admitted to Wenham Church, with his father and mother.

On 27 May, 1663, admitted freeman.

On 8 August, 1665, wife Sarah died; four children.

Gott married at Lynn, 25 December, 1665, second wife, Lydia, daughter of William Clark, of Lynn; four children. She was born 31 October, 1642.

In 1693, Charles Gott, Lieutentant of train-band.

He died 11 February, 1707–8; widow Lydia died 20 February, 1717–18.

Children — by first wife, Sarah:

1. Bethiah, born 24 April, 1661; died young.
2. Charles, born 7 August, 1662.
3. Sarah, born 4 January, 1663–4; died young.
4. Sarah, born 28 December, 1664.

By second wife, Lydia:

5. JOHN, born 8 November, 1668.
6. Debora, born 16 October, 1670.
7. Bethiah, born 16 July, 1674.
8. Samuel, birth unknown.

Lieut. JOHN GOTT, of Wenham; son of Lieut. Charles. Born 8 November, 1668. Married, 19 July, 1693, Rebekah, daughter of Samuel Tarbox, of Lynn; she was born 8 August, 1672.

In 1704, John Gott drew second lot in division of swamp land

His will, dated 21 January, 1722-3, gives son Benjamin "ye sum of £200 in silver money, or in good bills of credit," etc., "and they [his elder brothers, John and Samuel,] shall find him with good and sufficient clothing during the time he is to live with Dr. Wallis, as may appear by his indenture," etc.; "said £200 to be paid when he arrives at the age of twenty-one years."

John Gott died 25 January, 1722-3; gravestone in Wenham. Widow Rebekah probably married 14 October, 1723, second husband, William Fairfield, in Wenham.

Children:

1. John.
2. Samuel, born 30 November, 1695.
3. Lydia, born 17 March, 1698-9.
4. BENJAMIN, born 13 March, 1705-6.

Dr. BENJAMIN GOTT, of Marlboro; son of John. Born at Wenham, 13 March, 1705-6; being the youngest of four children.

In his youth he was indentured to "Dr. Wallis," perhaps Dr. Samuel Wallis, a physician of Ipswich, probably to study medicine. Benjamin's father died during the indenture; and in his will, dated 21 January, 1722-3, he provided for his son's maintenance during his study, and that he should receive £200 on attaining the age of twenty-one years.

Gott removed to Marlboro, and on 20 January, 1728, married Sarah, daughter of Rev. Robert Breck. He practiced medicine in Marlboro, accumulating some property, purchasing at different times parcels of real estate.

His wife, Sarah, died 10 April, 1740, aged twenty-eight, and is buried in Marlboro; six children. Dr. Gott married second wife, Lydia Ward, 5 October, 1740; she died 11 October, 1745 (gravestone), aged forty-three.

Dr. Gott died 25 July, 1751, aged forty-six. A notice of his death appeared in the Boston *News Letter*, 1 August, 1751, in which he is called a man of great learning, peculiarly faithful to his patients, moderate in his charges, and charitable to the poor. It is said he refreshed his knowledge of Latin by reading in the Latin Bible to his family every day.

Children — by first wife, Sarah:

1. Sarah.
2. ANNA, born 8 January, 1731; married Dr. Samuel Brigham.
3. Rebekah.
4. Benjamin.
5. Elizabeth.
6. John.

By second wife, Lydia.

7. Martha, born 11 September, 1741.

CLARK.

William.
Lydia, married Charles Gott.

WILLIAM CLARK, of Lynn, 1640. Immigrant. Wife, Mary, parentage unknown; eight children.

Will made 1679; died 5 March 1683. Widow, Mary, died 19 August, 1693.

Children:

1. LYDIA, born 31 October, 1642; married Charles Gott.
2. Hannah.
3. Sarah.
4. Mary.
5. William.
6. Elizabeth, born 6 October, 1652.
7. Martha, born 15 April, 1655.
8. John, born 2 January, 1659.

TARBOX.

John.
Samuel.
Rebecca, married Lieut. John Gott.

JOHN TARBOX, of Lynn, 1639. Immigrant.
First appears on Lynn records as plaintiff in a jury trial for

debt, 25 June, 1639, against Daniel Salmon; awarded 27s. damages and 11s. costs.

Name of wife unknown; four children.

In 1664, with others, inventoried estate of George Fraile. A farmer, and engaged 1656 in iron works.

Will, made 25 November, 1673, mentions two sons, John and Samuel. He died 26 May, 1674; his wife survived him.

Children:

1. Rebekah, born in England.
2. Jonathan, born in England; died 1654.
3. John, born 1645, in America.
4. SAMUEL, born 1647; married Rebekah Armitage.

Ensign SAMUEL TARBOX, son of John. Born 1647. Married first wife, 14 November, 1665, Rebekah, daughter Godfrey Armitage; six children. Tarbox was a soldier in King Philip's War, 1676–7, and while he was absent on service his wife died 4 or 7 March, 1676–7. His name appears in Captain Gardiner's Company as of Salem; and he is credited 29 February, 1675–6 with £3. 9s. 3d. for services.

He married second wife 16 October, 1678, Experience Look; twelve children.

In 1685, with others, petitioned General Court for remuneration for losses in Indian War, and on 3 June, 1685, was granted land in what was afterwards Worcester County.

On 16 August, 1715, he died, leaving all his property to his wife, Experience, who went to live with her son, Thomas, in Wenham, where she died 2 March, 1738, in her eighty-fifth year; gravestone in Wenham.

Children — by first wife, Rebekah:

1. Samuel, born 20 June, 1666.
2. Jonathan, born 3 July, 1668.
3. Godfrey, born 16 August, 1670.
4. REBEKAH, born 8 August, 1672; married Lieutenant John Gott.

5. Sarah, born 15 October, 1674.
6. Mary, born 21 February, 1676.

By wife, Experience.

7. Experience, born 1 or 10 September, 1679.
8. Hannah, born 12 March, 1681.
9. John, born 8 March, 1683.
10. Thomas, born 8 June, 1684.
11. Joseph, } born 8 January, 1685-6.
12. Elizabeth, }
13. Benjamin, born 23 January, 1686-7.
14. Mary, born 20 January, 1689.
15. Samuel, born ———— 1693.
16. Ebenezer, born 1 August, 1695.
17. Mehitable, born 12 June, 1697.
18. Joseph, born 6 March, 1699.

ARMITAGE.
Godfrey.
Rebekah, married Samuel Tarbox.

GODFREY ARMITAGE, of Lynn, 1630. Immigrant; a tailor. His brother Joseph, in 1661, made affidavit that he and Godfrey had eighty acres assigned to them in the division of Lynn lands. Freeman, 14 March, 1638-9.

In 1643, September, he signed petition of Jane, wife of brother Joseph, for a continuance to her of the license to "keep an ordinary;" the petition with his fac-simile autograph may be found in the N. E. H. G. Reg., 1879. Godfrey removed to Boston, and, about 1644, married Sarah, daughter of William and Rebekah Webb; two children.

About 1650 he married second wife, Mary, daughter of John Cogswell, Senior, of Ipswich; she was born 1619. Her brother, John Cogswell, wrote from London, 30 March, 1653, praying his father to help his "brother William and his brother Armitage," in the payment of £100., which he had "written to Armitage to pay for him because he lived in Boston." John Cogswell, Junior, died abroad; will of 13 December, 1652, proved 27 September, 1653, made brother William and brother Armitage executors.

Armitage appeared in the settlement of several estates; as appraiser 1652, estate John Roberts; 1654, John Avery; 1655, Nathaniel Souther; 1662, William Brown; as debtor, 1652, to estate of Captain Bozone Allen; as creditor, 1659, of estate of John Maynard; 1664, of Andrew Cloade; and in 1663 estate of John Stone owed "Armatage the Taylor."

About December, 1654, Rebekah Webb died, leaving all her property to her grand-child, Rebekah Armitage, Godfrey's daughter; will mentions Godfrey, and he appears on the records as overseer.

In 1669, he was overseer of will of Elizabeth Bitfield, who left him 50*s.* as a token "of love;" also, 20*s.* to Sam. Armitage. The same year he made his own will, leaving a legacy to his "daughter, Rebekah Tarbox." I have no record of his death.

Children — by wife, Sarah:

Samuel, born 7 October, 1645; died young.
REBECCA, married Samuel Tarbox.

By wife Mary:

Samuel, born 14 April, 1651.

WEBB.

William.
Sarah, married Godfrey Armitage.

WILLIAM WEBB, of Roxbury. Immigrant. Freeman, 25 May, 1636. On Rev. John Eliot's record of members of Roxbury Church. On early Roxbury records, list of persons and estates: William Webb, nineteen acres, four persons, estate £2.

Wife, Rebekah; parentage unknown.

In 1640, son Joseph born, 19 August.

In 1643, "8 mo., goodwife Web" disciplined by Roxbury Church.

Rebekah was restored to communion, recommended to Boston Church, and admitted there with her husband, 7 April, 1644. In December of same year, William Webb was buried.

In April, 1653, Rebekah sold her Roxbury estate.

In 1654, December 10, she made her will, leaving her grandchild, Rebekah Armitage, sole heir of her estate; mentioning "hir father Godfrey Armitage," and in another place, "sonne Armitage," and again, "sonne in lawe." Estate inventoried 22 December, 1654; will proved 23 February, 1654–5; Armitage, one of the overseers. They deposed 16 March, 1654, and gave bond for £180; Armitage here made his mark.

Children:

SARAH, married Godfrey Armitage.
Joseph, born 19 August, 1640.

BRECK.

Edward.
John.
Robert.
Sarah, married Benjamin Gott.

EDWARD BRECK, of Dorchester, 1636. Immigrant. Born probably in Lancashire, England, about 1595. Married in England, probably about 1617, name of wife unknown; four children, born in England. Emigrated from Ashton, with wife, one daughter, and son Robert. They sailed with Rev. Richard Mather from Bristol, arriving in Boston 7 August, 1635. Settled in Dorchester, joining the church in 1636. He was a man of education, and seems to have brought some means from England.

On 20 June, 1638, bought lands of Thomas Treadwell; consideration, £51.

On 22 May, 1639, freeman.

On 18 February, 1641, Frances Burre conveyed land to Edward Breck of Dorchester, yeoman; consideration, £20.

In 1641, conveyed land to town for support of "free school."

In 1642, 1645, 1646, Selectman.

In 1643, bought wild land in what is now Lancaster.

In 1645, on committee to build meeting house in Dorchester.

Granted water-privilege on Smelt Brook, on condition of building a mill, which he did; same year his wife died.

In 1646, received letter now extant from John Wood, of Ashton, in England.

In 1647, married second wife, Isabel, widow of John Rigby; four children.

In 1653, appointed by General Court one of the prudential managers of the new settlement at Lancaster.

In 1654, petitioned General Court that Lancaster be made a township, but he never made it his home; sold house and lot in Boston to his son Robert.

In 1655, 1656, Selectman in Dorchester.

In 1655, engaged Ichabod Wiswall to teach the school, to be paid two-thirds in wheat, pease, or barley; one-third in Indian corn.

In 1655, petitioned General Court to remit fine for not serving as constable; petition denied.

In 1655, wrote letter to Church in Rainforth, Lancashire, England, to confirm their faith; condemning the Quakers; letter printed in London; copy in British Museum.

In 1657, paid his school-tax in pease.

Will made 30 October, 1662; he died 2 November, 1662. Inventory Dorchester property, £746; Lancaster property, £81; debts, £126. The inventory mentions "books," apparently few. His widow, Isabel, married in 1663 Anthony Fisher, and died 21 June, 1673.

Children—by first wife—all born in England:

1. Daughter, name unknown; died in England.
2. Robert.
3. Daughter, name unknown.
4. Elinor.

By wife, Isabel—born in America:

5. Mary, baptized 1648.
6. JOHN, born 1651.
7. Elizabeth.
8. Susanna.

Capt. JOHN BRECK, of Dorchester, son of Edward. Born about 1651. A tanner; also other business. Married about 1671 Susanna ———; she was born in 1648; parentage unknown.

He is always called Captain; owned a cider-mill.

In 1680, built a vessel; was made a feoffee of school land; on committee to repair school-house.

In 1681, disciplined for voting in church meeting when he was not in full communion.

In 1682, widow Elizabeth Gray licensed to keep an ordinary, on condition that Breck shall see that it is kept according to law.

In 1683, on committee to lay out school land.

In 1686, Selectman.

In 1687, again on committee about school land.

In 1688, Selectman again.

In 1690, admitted freeman; filed inventory of estate of Thomas Tolman, Senior; on committee to seat the people in the meeting-house.

Will made 4 February, 1691-2; and he died 17 February, 1691-2; age, forty; leaving several young children. His will provides that "one of my sons be brought up to learning," also "my children I will to be well educated." His son Robert graduated at Harvard College, 1700, and became a minister. Estate foots up £1359; "books £2-10." Widow Susanna died 8 February, 1711; aged, sixty-four.

Children:

1. Jemima, born 17 April, 1672.
2. Edward, born 7 April, 1674.
3. Elizabeth, born 20 September, 1676.
4. Susanna, born 9 November, 1678.

5. John, born 22 December, 1680.
6. ROBERT, born 7 December, 1682. H. C., 1700. Minister in Marlboro.
7. Nathaniel, born 1 December, 1684.
8. Hannah, died an infant.
9. Hannah, born 17 February, 1688.
10. Samuel, born 14 September, 1690.

Rev. ROBERT BRECK, of Marlboro, son of Captain John. Born in Dorchester, 7 December, 1682. His father died when he was a child; graduated from Harvard College, 1700; preached a short time at Newtown, Long Island; returned to Massachusetts, and was ordained at Marlboro, 25 October, 1704.

On 8 September, 1707, married Elizabeth Wainwright, of Haverhill, probably daughter of Major Simon Wainwright; six children. "He was a man of strong natural powers, clear head and solid judgment;" the Marlboro Church had been rent by dissension, but though only twenty-two years old, he united it into a strong, solid parish. He was a man of learning and read Greek and Hebrew fluently.

The "Marlboro Association" of ministers, which included seven adjoining towns, was organized at his house 5 June, 1725, and he was the central figure during his life. At the ordination of Rev. Mr. Frink, of Rutland, in 1727, he presided over the council at which Simon Davis, Senior, was a delegate.

Mr. Breck died much lamented 6 January, 1731, after a lingering illness and much suffering, endured with great patience; a monument stands over his remains in Marlboro. His death was noticed in the Boston *News Letter*, 12 January, 1731. We have in print four sermons from his pen, and three funeral discourses preached at his death by his fellow-ministers. His two sons graduated at Harvard College. His widow, Elizabeth, died 8 June, 1736, in her fifty-second year; gravestone in Marlboro.

In his will made 22 December, 1730, Breck gives his son-in-law, Dr. Gott, two acres land as recompense for "instructing my son Robert in the rules of physic," also "Ten pounds worth of books out of my library;" also to daughter, Sarah Gott, "my silver tankard," and one cow. This Robert became minister at Springfield.

Children:

1. Elizabeth, born 23 September, 1709.
2. SARAH, born 10 October, 1711; married Dr. Benjamin Gott, of Marlboro.
3. Robert, born 25 July, 1713. H. C., 1730.
4. Hannah, born 10 February, 1717.
5. Samuel, born 17 May, 1723. H. C., 1741.
6. Anna, born 13 March, 1725.

WAINWRIGHT.

Francis.
Simon.
Elizabeth, married Rev. Robert Breck.

FRANCIS WAINWRIGHT, of Ipswich, 1638. Immigrant. Born in England.

In 1638, at Ipswich, Mass., a merchant of prominence. Wife, Philippa ————; eight children.

On 19 December, 1648, assessed £o. 4s. od. at Ipswich, to pay Major Denison as "leader of the company."

In 1664, corporal.

On 9 October, 1669, wife Philippa died.

On 31 May, 1671, admitted freeman.

On 18 February, 1678, on list of persons in Ipswich entitled to "comonage."

At some time after 1669, he married second wife, Hannah, parentage unknown.

He died at Salem, 19 May, 1692.

Will provides for widow Hannah, daughters Mary, Martha, Mehitable, and Elizabeth, and children of daughter Sarah and son John.

His widow married Daniel Epes of Salem.

Children—all by first wife:

1. John, born about 1648; had two sons, graduates H. C.
2. Sarah.
3. Mary.
4. Martha.
5. SIMON, born about 1656.
6. Mehitable.
7. Elizabeth.
8. Francis, born 25 August 1664. H. C., 1686.

The descendants of Francis Wainwright for the next two generations form a remarkable family, noted for its wealth, its military spirit, and the extraordinary number of college-bred men.

Capt. SIMON WAINWRIGHT, of Haverhill, 1684, son of Francis. Born in Ipswich, about 1656. A prominent merchant; Captain.

The details of his life are much confused; three wives are mentioned.

First, Sarah Gilbert, parentage unknown.

Second, Anne, daughter of Daniel Pierce, of Newbury. She was born 22 May, 1666. Pierce's will dated 12 October, 1701, proved 8 May, 1704, mentions "son-in-law Simon Wainwright and grandson John Wainwright."

Third wife, Mary, widow of Thomas Silver.

Wainwright was killed by the Indians in their attack on Haverhill, 29 August, 1708.

Children—by wife, Sarah:

1. Sarah, born 17 July, 1682. Married 7 February, 1699, Charles Frost. She died 5 June, 1714.
2. ELIZABETH, born 1684 or '85. Married Rev. Robert Breck, of Marlboro. She may possibly have been daughter of wife Anne.

By wife Anne:

3. John, born probably 1688, or 1689. H. C., 1709. Died 1739.
Probably other children.

BANCROFT.

Thomas.
Thomas.
Samuel.
Samuel.
Aaron.
Eliza, married John Davis.

Lieut. THOMAS BANCROFT, of Reading. Immigrant. Born about 1622; perhaps the Thomas Bancroft mentioned in Records of Cheadle, Stafford County, England, as baptized 10 February, 1622. Savage and others identify him with Thomas, son of John and Jane Barcroft, of Lynn, 1632–1638, but there is no evidence of such connection; on the contrary, there is reason to think the Lynn Barcrofts were another family, and emigrated to Connecticut before 1648.

The first sure mention of him is his marriage, when twenty-five years old, at Dedham, 31 January, 1647, to Alice, daughter of Michael Bacon; she had one child, which died in infancy, and she died 29 January, 1648. Michael Bacon, in his will, made 14 February, 1648, gives 20s. to Thomas Bancroft, his son-in-law.

Bancroft married second wife at Dedham, 15 September, 1648, Elizabeth, daughter of Michael Metcalf. She was born in England, 4 October, 1626.

Probably about this time Bancroft moved to Reading, as on 29 September, 1648, his name appears on the first list of church members there; in 1652, he sold his property in Dedham.

On 25 December, 1662, wife Elizabeth was dismissed from Dedham Church to Reading Church. On 12 May, 1663, Joan Marshall disciplined by Reading Church for speaking "offensive words against Sister Bancroft."

In 1664, Michael Metcalf left his daughter, Elizabeth Bancroft, £5 in his will.

In 1670, Bancroft purchased sixty acres near Beaver Dam, now Lynnfield; same year appraised estate of John Pearson; also estate of Wm. Stewart.

On 16 October, 1672, Richard Walker for £36 conveyed to Bancroft twenty acres in Reading.

On 29 March, 1675, Bancroft conveyed to his son Thomas twenty acres upland in Reading.

In 1678, freeman at Reading.

On 10 September, 1678, Nathaniel Cowdery conveyed to him eleven acres in Reading.

In 1681, stating his age at "about fifty-eight," he made affidavit, that about 1655 he hired a farm of Samuel Bennett.

In 1683, appraised estate of Walter Cranston.

In 1688, subscribed £5 for a new church. He seems to have taken little part in town affairs.

He died intestate, 19 August, 1691, aged sixty-nine; gravestone in Reading (now Wakefield).

On 23 November, 1691, agreement for partition of estate signed by widow and children; Thomas acknowledges having received his share before his father's death. In this instrument the men sign their full names; the women make their mark. Inventory, 23 September, 1691: Real estate, £267; personal, £117; books, 40s.

Widow Elizabeth died 1 May, 1711.

Children—all by wife, Elizabeth:

1. THOMAS, born at Dedham, 14 July, 1649.
2. Elizabeth, born at Dedham, 21 January, 1650; died young.
3. John, born at Dedham, 3 March, 1651; died young.
4. Elizabeth, born at Reading, 7 December, 1653.
5. John, born at Reading, 3 March, 1656.
6. Sarah, born 14 March, 1657; died young.
7. Ralph, born at Reading, 20 August, 1660; died young.
8. Raham, born at Reading, 27 June, 1662.
9. Sarah, born at Reading, 1 April, 1665.
10. Ebenezer, born at Lynn, 26 April, 1667.
11. Mary, born at Lynn, 16 May, 1670.

Capt. THOMAS BANCROFT (2d) of Reading, son of Thomas. Born at Dedham, 14 July, 1649; parents removed to Reading soon after.   A quaint story of his wonderful recovery from small-pox when young is told in Mather's "Magnalia."

He married 10 April, 1673, Sarah, daughter of Jonathan Poole; she was born 11 July, 1656.

In 1675, he was Captain of Reading Infantry Company, and took an active part in the Indian wars.   Selectman several years between 1685 and 1716.

In 1676, with Jonathan Poole, petitioned Governor and Council to strengthen the outlying towns.

On 10 February, 1680, wife Sarah received bequest of six and one-half acres upland in Reading from her father, Jonathan Poole.

In 1686, assessed 2/6 to pay Indians for land.

In 1688, subscribed £7 towards a new church.

In 1694, chosen Assessor; same year spoken of as owning a saw-mill.

In 1696, engaged in an effort to relieve Hilton's garrison besieged by Indians; lost eight or nine of his men.

Deacon of the First Church, Reading.   Died 12 June, 1718, aged sixty-nine.

Will, dated 1714, gives "all my history books to be divided among my three sons equally; my divinity books among all my children, not including my Bible, Clark's Annotations, which I give to my son Thomas."

On 3 January, 1720–1, widow Sarah in list of church members First Church, Reading.   She died "27 May, 1723, in ye 67 year of her age."

Children:
1. Thomas, born 8 September, 1673.
2. Jonathan, died young.
3. Sarah, born 28 December, 1675.
4. Mehitable, born 1 February, 1678.
5. Jonathan, born 4 October, 1681.
6. Raham, born 14 February, 1684.
7. Judith, born 7 March, 1687.

8. Samuel, born 18 December, 1691; died young.
9. SAMUEL, born 26 December, 1693.
10. Elizabeth, born 22 June, 1696.

Capt. SAMUEL BANCROFT (1st), of Reading, son of Thomas, Junior. Born 26 December, 1693.

Married 22 November, 1713, first wife, Sarah, daughter of Samuel Lamson; she was born in 1689. He inherited his father's house in Reading.

On 3 January, 1720–1, he and Sarah, his wife, are on the list of members of the First Church, Reading. Wife Sarah died 3 January, 1733, aged forty-three. He married 22 August, 1733, second wife, Sarah Leathe. Married 24 August, 1761, third wife, Mehitable Fitch.

Captain of Reading Infantry Company, and served in the Indian Wars; owned slaves, Cato and Phyllis.

Selectman, five years between 1730 and 1753; Representative to General Court.

In 1737, he was on a committee in relation to the Mystic Bridge.

In 1765, owned dwelling-house in First Parish, Reading (now Wakefield). Eaton says it stood on what is now Fremont Street.

In 1771, on list of voters First Parish.

Wife Mehitable died 12 April, 1772.

He died 13 July, 1772, aged seventy-nine.

Children — all by wife, Sarah:

1. SAMUEL, born 21 July, 1715.
2. William, born 1717.
3. Edmund, born 1718.
4. Nathaniel, born 1720.
5. Sarah, born 1722.
6. Jacob, born 1723.
7. Jeremiah, born 1725.
8. Caleb, born 1731.

     Only four of these survived him.

Esquire SAMUEL BANCROFT (2d), son of Samuel. Born 21 July, 1715.

Married 30 October, 1735, Lydia, daughter of Nathaniel Parker; she was born February, 1716.

"He lived on West street, near the Woburn line;" owned the place in 1765, and gave it to his son Caleb. (Eaton's Hist. Reading.)

On 2 November, 1758, chosen Deacon First Parish, Reading. Selectman five years between 1757 and 1766; Justice of the Peace; Representative to the General Court; Major of Regiment.

In 1769, with others, made unsuccessful effort to change location of new meeting-house First Parish, Reading.

In 1769, the disaffected persons formed new parish, called the Third Parish; Samuel Bancroft, Esq., chosen Clerk; Deacon Samuel Bancroft one of Assessors.

In 1771, name in list of voters Third Parish; in 1773, he signed report settling matters of dispute between First and Third Parishes.

In 1773, on committee which made report to the town on political grievances arising between Great Britain and the Colonies.

In 1774, on another committee renewing the same protest.

Eaton's History of Reading names among "the able and wise men" brought out by the exigencies of the Revolution, "Samuel Bancroft, Esq., the wise counselor and able speaker, then in the vale of years."

In 1774, had three slaves; in 1776, by written instrument, promised freedom in three years to slave Cato.

Died 15 or 25 November, 1782, aged sixty-seven. Widow Lydia died November, 1813, aged ninety-seven years and nine months. Dr. Jos. Allen says of Bancroft, "He was a man of distinguished abilities, of great benevolence and compassion," and of his wife, "She was a pious and affectionate woman."

Children:

1. Samuel, born 1736.
2. Lydia, born 1738..
3. Sarah, born 1740.

4. Mary, born 1742.
5. Mehitable, born 1744.
6. Elizabeth, born 1746.
7. Anne, born 1749.
8. Edmund, born 1751.
9. Caleb, born 1753.
10. AARON, born 10 November, 1755. H. C., 1778.
11. Lucy, born 1758.

Nathan Weston, Chief Justice of the Supreme Court of Maine, was the son of Elizabeth Bancroft; and Melville Weston Fuller, present Chief Justice of the Supreme Court of the United States, is her great-grandson.

Rev. AARON BANCROFT, son of Esquire Samuel. Born in Reading, Mass., 10 November, 1755. Entered Harvard College 1774. When the college exercises were suspended in 1775, he joined the minute men from Reading and marched to the relief of the army at Cambridge; returning to his studies, he graduated in 1778; prepared for the ministry; began preaching in 1779. In 1780, by permission of the Executive Council, he went to Nova Scotia, where he preached at different points for three years; returning home in 1783, he preached in Worcester and other places. On the death of Rev. Mr. Maccarty, at Worcester, in 1784, a portion of the parish wished to retain him as the pastor of the First Church, but the town refused to settle him on account of his Arminian views; whereupon sixty-seven men formed a new parish and made him their minister. For many years he had a bitter struggle against straitened circumstances and hostile feelings; but he remained at his post until his death, fifty-three years later.

He was ordained 1 February, 1786; married 24 October, 1786, Lucretia, daughter Hon. John Chandler (then a refugee); she was born 9 June, 1765.

He took an active part in educational and religious matters outside of his pastoral duties; received the degree of D. D. from Harvard College, 1810; was Trustee of Leicester Academy from

1800 to 1831, and President many years; President of the Worcester County Bible Society; President of the American Unitarian Association from its formation in 1825 to 1836, and of the Society for Promoting Christian Knowledge; Vice-President of the Worcester and Middlesex Missionary Society; of the American Antiquarian Society from 1816 to 1832; Fellow of the American Academy of Arts and Sciences; and member of other societies.

He published in 1807 a life of Washington, which was twice reprinted, and in 1822 a volume of sermons which attracted much attention, also many sermons in pamphlet form.

Mrs. Bancroft died 27 April, 1839, nearly 74 years old. During her life her brilliant social qualities had been greatly admired, and after her death her active benevolence and her devoted self-sacrifice were held in grateful remembrance.

After her funeral Dr. Bancroft never left the house, and died 19 August following, in his 84th year. His memory was cherished for "his warm heart, courteous manners, and devoted fidelity in all relations of public and private life."

Children:

1. Henry, born 8 October, 1787.
2. John Chandler, born 27 June, 1789.
3. ELIZA, born 17 February, 1791; married John Davis.
4. Mary, born 1 June, 1793.
5. Caroline, born 23 April, 1795.
6. Thomas Chandler, born 28 December, 1796.
7. Jane Putnam, born 12 November, 1798.
8. George, born 3 October, 1800.
9. Lucretia, born 19 May, 1803.
10. Charles, born 18 February, 1805.
11. Sarah, born 5 June, 1806.
12. Dorothy, born 10 August, 1807; died young.
13. Anne, born 31 October, 1809.

George Bancroft was the well known historian. He graduated at Harvard College, 1817; received also Ph. D., Göttingen; LL. D., Harvard, and many other honorary degrees; member of many learned societies; Secretary of the Navy; Minister Plen-ipotentiary to Great Britain and Germany.

———

METCALF.

Michael.
Elizabeth, married Thomas Bancroft.

MICHAEL METCALF, of Dedham, 1637. Immigrant. Born in 1586, at Tatterford, County Norfolk, England. A dornock weaver at Norwich; made freeman of Norwich, England, 21 June, 1618; married in Waynham, 13 October, 1616, Sarah ———; she was born on 17 June, 1593.

Persecuted by Bishop Wren for non-conformity, he took ship alone at London, 17 September, 1636, for New England; driven back by storms to Plymouth; he sailed from Yarmouth, 15 April, 1637, with wife, nine children, and servant. Landed at Boston; admitted freeman at Dedham, 14 July, 1637; joined church 1639; Selectman, 1641; on Committee to build new meeting-house. Wife Sarah died 30 November, 1644 (21 February, 1645, Savage).

He married 13 August, 1645, second wife, Mary, widow of Thomas Pigge. In 1656, when seventy years old, he agreed to teach the children of Dedham to read and write; consideration, £20, to be paid in grain.

On 22 May, 1664, he witnessed will of Joshua Kent, of Ded-ham. He died 27 December, 1664; will proved 1 February, 1664-5; inventory, £364. 18s. 5d.; will disposes of his books.

Children — by wife, Sarah — all born in England.

1. Michael, died young.
2. Mary.
3. Michael.
4. John.
5. Sarah.
6. ELIZABETH, born 4 October, 1626; married Thos. Bancroft.
7. Martha.
8. Thomas.

9. Ann; died young.
10. Jane.
11. Rebeka.

Memoranda in N. E. H. G. Register.
Letter of Michael Metcalf, 1636.   Register, 1862, p. 279.
Metcalf Family.   Register, April, 1852.
Metcalf's Will.   Register, April, 1852, p. 172.
Metcalf's Will.   Register, May, 1853, p. 230.

POOLE.

John.
Jonathan.
Sarah, married Thomas Bancroft.

JOHN POOLE, of Cambridge, 1632.   Immigrant.   Wife, Margaret.

At Lynn before 1638, where he owned 200 acres.   About 1640, on the Lynn town rates he is taxed £1. 15s.

At Reading before 1644; that year he was assigned a water privilege and built the first sawmill and gristmill.

In 1648, chosen Surveyor of Highways.

In 1652, in allotment of new lands he drew twenty acres; again in 1658, upland, 206 acres.

Wife Margaret, died 29 April, 1662.

In 1664, with others, he received more land.

In 1665, his minister rates were £2. 14s. 5d.

In 1666, assigned land in Great Swamp.

On 14 February, 1666-7, made his will, and died 1 April, 1667.   He was one of the wealthiest men in Reading.

Children:

JONATHAN, born 1634.
Mary.

Captain JONATHAN POOLE, of Reading, son of John. Born 1634. Married, about 1655, Judith ———.

Judith Poole is on first list of church members in Reading.

In 1658, alloted 145 acres land.

In 1661, with others, contracted to make repairs on church; same year appointed to lay out land.

Selectman 1662–64; 1668–74, 1676, 1677.

In 1667, on list of house-owners; same year he inherited the homestead from his father: he also owned much land besides.

In 1668, agreement with town for maintenance of watermill.

In 1675, he joined the militia in King Philip's War; was Captain of Reading Company, acting in this capacity under Major Appleton at Hadley; his services were much valued, and he was President of the Council of War in the winter of 1675–76.

The above account of his military record is from Eaton's History of Reading.

It is given in the Genealogical Register of July, 1887, as follows: In 1671, appointed Quartermaster; in 1674, made Cornet of the "Three County Troop"; in 1675, King Philip's War broke out; Poole served as Cornet under Lieut. Hasey; 30 September, 1675, he was in command of garrison at Quaboag; in command of a company at the defense of Hatfield; then appointed to a captaincy, and placed in command of the garrison forces in the "Connecticut towns."

Relieved at his own request 24 June, 1676; credited 24 June, 1676, as follows: Jonathan Poole, Captain, £5. 0s. 0d.; Jonathan Poole, Captain, £44. 5s. 4d.

In 1675, petitioned General Court to open the river for fish.

In 1676, with Thomas Bancroft, petitioned Governor and Council to strengthen the outlying towns; his name appears on other petitions to the Colonial authorities.

In 1677, Representative to the General Court; he was also Justice of the Peace. He died 24 December, 1678, in his forty-fourth year.

Children:

1. SARAH, born 11 July, 1656; married Thomas Bancroft.
2. Judith, born 1658.
3. Mary, born 1660; died young.
4. Mary, born 1662.
5. John, born 1665.
6. Jonathan, born 1667.
7. Thomas, born 1673.
8. William, born 1677.
9. Elizabeth, born 1678.

LAMSON.

William.
Samuel.
Sarah, married Samuel Bancroft.

WILLIAM LAMSON, of Ipswich. Immigrant. Freeman, 17 May, 1637. Wife, Sarah, and eight children.

On 19 December, 1648, taxed £0 2s. 0d. at Ipswich town meeting to be paid Major Denison as "Leader." He died 1 February, 1659, leaving eight children. His farm of 300 acres in Ipswich is still owned by his descendants. Widow Sarah married 10 April, 1661, Thomas Hartshorne, of Reading, and undoubtedly moved thither with her children.

Children:

1. SAMUEL.
2. Joseph, born about 1658.
3. Sarah, and five others.

SAMUEL LAMSON, of Reading, probably son of William, of Ipswich, whose widow married in 1661, Thomas Hartshorne, of Reading, and with her children came to Reading.

In 1675, Lamson enlisted in King Philip's War; he is credited with service as follows: On 29 February, 1675-6, £3. 7s. 0d. for service under Capt. Davenport and Capt. Ting, and on 24 June, 1676, £2. 19s. 6d. for service under Capt. Joseph Syll.

In 1676, Lamson married Mary, daughter of Richard Nichols.

In 1677, applied to be admitted as freeman, "being in full communion in the church at Reading;" admitted 23 May, 1677.

In 1686, assessed sixpence to pay Indians for land bought by the town.

In 1688, subscribed £4 towards new meeting-house.

In 1692, his "minister tax" was £0. 14s. 2d.

Lamson died in 1692.

Children:

1. Samuel, born 1677.
2. Mary, born 1678.
3. Ebenezer, died young.
4. William, died young.
5. Joanna, born 1682.
6. Ebenezer, born 1685.
7. John, born 1686.
8. SARAH, born 1689; married Capt. Samuel Bancroft.
9. Elizabeth, born 1691.

NICHOLS.

Richard.
Mary, married Samuel Lamson.

RICHARD NICHOLS, of Ipswich, 1648. Immigrant; later of Reading. Wife, Anna ———.

His name first appears in Reading on the division of the Great Swamp in 1666, where his proportion is based on his "minister tax" of 1665, which was £1. 5s. 2d.

In 1667, in list of house-owners in Reading.

Made will 19 November, 1674; and died 22 November, 1674.

Widow Anna died 1692.

Children:

MARY; married Samuel Lamson.
Thomas.
John, born 1651.
James, born about 1658.
Richard.
Hannah.

PARKER.

Thomas.
Nathaniel.
Nathaniel.
Lydia, married Samuel Bancroft.

Deacon THOMAS PARKER, of Lynn and Reading. Immigrant; came in the Susan and Ellen, 1635, aged thirty. Freeman, 17 May, 1637; married, probably about 1637, Amy———; parentage unknown. Removed to Reading by 1644; one of its founders; appointed Deacon, 1645; he and his wife on first list of members First Church, about 1650.

In 1652, drew by lot fifteen acres on "the Playne"; and in 1658, drew land on Ipswich River.

Selectman, 1661, 1665–67, 1669.

In 1665, appointed "Commissioner for ending small causes."

In 1667, on list of house owners, "Thomas Parker (2)."

In 1675, with others petitioned the General Court to open the river for fish; and again, in 1677, in behalf of Capt. Poole.

In 1678, joined in another petition respecting church matters.

On 3 April, 1683, made his will; probated 18 December, same year. His burial slab at Reading states that he died 12 August, 1683, aged about seventy-four, which is inconsistent with his age as given above.

Widow Amy died 15 January, 1690.

Children:

1. Hananiah, born 1638.
2. Thomas.

3. Joseph, born 1642; died young.
4. Joseph, born 1645; died young.
5. Mary, born 1647.
6. Martha, born 1649.
7. NATHANIEL, born 16 May, 1651.
8. Sarah, born 1653; died young.
9. Jonathan, born 1656.
10. Sarah, born 1658.
11. John.

Ensign NATHANIEL PARKER, of Reading; son of Thomas. Born 16 May, 1651.

Married 1677, Bethiah, daughter of John Polly, of Roxbury; she was born 12 February, 1659; settled in West Parish, Reading.

In 1686, assessed £0. 2s. 6d. for lands bought by the town from the Indians.

In 1691, freeman; same year "minister tax," £1. 4s 6d.

In 1692, allotted lands in "Great Swamp."

Selectman, 1695–97, 1705–14, and 1727.

In 1708, Ensign Parker added to school committee.

On 3 January, 1720–1, Nathaniel Parker, Senior, and his wife on list of members First Church.

He died in 1737, aged eighty-seven.

Widow Bethiah died on 23 August, 1748, in her ninetieth year.

Children:

1. Bethiah, born 1678; died young.
2. NATHANIEL, born 4 December, 1679.
3. Stephen, born 1684; died young.
4. Bethiah, born 1685.
5. Susannah, born 1687.
6. Ebenezer, born 1689.
7. Stephen, born 1692.
8. Caleb, born 1694.
9. Timothy, born 1696.
10. Obadiah, born 1698.

11. Abigail, born 1699.
12. Amy, born 1701; died young.
13. Amy, born 1702.
14. Phineas, born 1704.

Lieut. NATHANIEL PARKER, of Reading; also called Nathaniel Parker, Jr., son of Nathaniel Parker, Senior. Born 4 December, 1679; married about 1701, Elizabeth ———; parentage unknown.

On 3 January, 1720-1, he and his wife are on the list of members of the First Church, Reading.

In 1728, Selectman.

In 1732, Rev. Mr. Brown, minister of First Church, died, and in 1733, Rev. Mr. Hobby was invited to succeed him; on bill of expenses at Rev. Mr. Brown's funeral is this item: "To Lt. Nathaniel Parker, for 5 qts. Rhom. 8*s.*"

In 1733, he was on the committee to confer with the Rev. Mr. Hobby.

This is the last mention I have found of him in the history of Reading; in 1765, his name is not on the list of house-owners.

Children:

1. Elizabeth, born 1703.
2. Phineas, born 1704.
3. Bethiah, born 1707.
4. Nathaniel, born 1710.
5. LYDIA, born 1716; married Samuel Bancroft.
6. Nathan, born 1719.
7. Mehitable, born 1721.
8. Caleb, born 1725.

POLLY.
John.
Bethiah, married Nathaniel Parker.

JOHN POLLY, of Roxbury.   Immigrant.   Born, 1617 or '18.
Married first wife, Susanna ———; parentage unknown; six
children.   She died 30 April, 1664.

Married second wife, Hannah ———; parentage unknown;
two children.   She died 8 June, 1684.

Married third wife, Jane Walter.

He died 2 April, 1689, aged seventy-one.

Widow Jane died 24 October, 1701.

Children — by wife, Susanna:

1. Mary, } twins, baptized 2 June, 1650.
2. Sarah, }
3. Hannah, baptized 15 February, 1652.
4. Abigail, baptized 4 June, 1654.
5. BETHIAH, born 12 February, 1659; married Nathaniel
   Parker.
6. Susannah, baptized 22 December, 1661.

By wife, Hannah.

7. Rebeka, born 7 August, 1668.
8. Joanna, born 7 March, 1670.

CHANDLER.

William.
John.
John.
John.
John.
Lucretia, married Aaron Bancroft.

WILLIAM CHANDLER, of Roxbury. Immigrant. Came over in 1637, with wife Annis and four children. She is supposed to have been the sister of Deacon George Alcock. Chandler took the freeman's oath in 1640.

They are spoken of as "leading a religious and godly life," but as very poor.

On the Roxbury Records he is credited with "1 goat, 1 kid"; and again with "22 acres, 7 persons."

He soon developed consumption, and died 19 January, 1642. During his last illness, through the kindness of his neighbors, "he never wanted that which was very plentiful and comfortable to him." He left a widow and five young children. She married 2 July, 1643, John Dane, with whose aid she was enabled to care for her young family. On Dane's death, she married 9 August, 1660, John Parmenter, and died 15 March, 1683. The church records lament her loss as "Old Mother Parminter, a blessed saint."

Children:

1. Hannah, born in England about 1629.
2. Thomas, born in England, 1630.
3. William, born in England.
4. JOHN, born in England about 1635.
5. Sarah, born in America.

DEACON JOHN CHANDLER (1st), of Woodstock; son of William. Born in England about 1635. Came to America with his parents 1637.

In 1642, his mother was by the death of her husband left destitute with five small children. In July, 1643, she married John Dane, who helped her to bring up her family.

We know nothing of John Chandler's early life till, on 16 February, 1658–9, he married Elizabeth, daughter of William Douglas. She was born in Ipswich 26 August, 1641.

Savage says Chandler was of Boston for some years, but on the 27 January, 1661, he was chosen to dig the graves at Roxbury. His wife joined the church at Roxbury, 28 May, 1665, and he followed her example, 13 April, 1679.

In 1684, being nearly fifty years old, he started out with others to settle New Roxbury, which is now Woodstock, Conn., being then part of Massaachusetts, and in 1686 he moved there with his family.

In 1689, he sold ten acres in Roxbury, "on which his mansion house standeth."

He took a prominent part in the new town; was Deacon of the church; Moderator of the town-meetings, and was repeatedly chosen Selectman.

He made his will 1 June, 1702, and died 15 April, 1703, at Woodstock, "aged about sixty-eight years," says his gravestone at Woodstock.

His estate was valued at £512, most of which was land and buildings.

Children:

1. John, born 4 March, 1659–60; died young.
2. Elizabeth, born 20 February, 1661.
3. JOHN, born 16 April, 1665.
4. Joseph, born 3 April, 1667; died young.
5. Hannah, born 8 September, 1669.
6. Mehitable, born 24 August, 1673.
7. Sarah, born 19 November, 1676.
8. Joseph, born 4 June, 1683.

Hon. JOHN CHANDLER (2d), of Woodstock; son of John (1st). Born at Roxbury, 16 April, 1665. Moved with his father into the wilderness at the settling of Woodstock in 1686.

In 1686 and 1688, assigned lands at Wappaquasset (Woodstock); in 1690, Town Clerk; also appointed to teach the children to read, write, and cipher; in 1692–3, again Town Clerk.

On 10 November, 1692, married Mary, daughter of Joshua Raymond, of New London; she was born 12 March, 1671–2.

In 1693–4, one of "Town Committee"; in 1694, Selectman.

Moved to New London, where he spent several years, and where, in 1698, he was licensed to keep a house of entertainment.

Returned to Woodstock, where he lived the rest of his life. In 1711, Representative to General Court of Massachusetts, and for several years thereafter.

Wife Mary died 8 April, 1711, aged thirty-nine; gravestone in Woodstock. Married, 14 November, 1711, second wife, Mrs. Esther Alcock.

In 1722, during the Indian War, which lasted some years, he commanded a company of scouts, with rank of Major; in 1724, made Colonel.

In 1731, when Worcester County was formed, he was made first Judge of Probate Court and Chief Justice of the Court of Common Pleas.

These offices and his rank of Colonel he held till his death in 1743.

In 1735, by appointment, he read an address to Governor Belcher and his council on their way to Albany to confer with the Six Nations. He was nearly forty years a Commissioner of the Peace, and for seven years was a member of his Majesty's Council.

He died in Woodstock, 10 August, 1743, in his seventy-ninth year.

His will made at Woodstock, 25 July, 1740, was proved at Worcester, 12 August, 1743. The inventory shows property amounting to about £8700 in the currency of that day.

Wife Esther was living in 1740, and probably survived him.

Children — all by first wife:

1. JOHN, born in New London, 18 October, 1693.
2. Joshua, born in New London, 9 February, 1695–6.
3. William, born in New London, 3 November, 1698.
4. Mary, born in New London, 30 April, 1700.
5. Elizabeth, born in Woodstock, 13 May, 1702.
6. Samuel, born in Woodstock, 5 January, 1703–4.
7. Sarah, born in Woodstock, 11 October, 1705.
8. Mehitable, born in Woodstock, 10 August, 1707.
9. Thomas, born in Woodstock, 23 July, 1709.
10. Hannah, born in Woodstock, 27 March, 1711.

JOHN CHANDLER (3d), of Worcester; son of John (2d). Born in New London, 10 or 18 October, 1693.

In his early years was a surveyor of land; surveyed and plotted the town of Pomfret; and assisted in surveying the line between Massachusetts and Connecticut in 1714.

Married, 23 October, 1716, at Gardiner's Island, Hannah, daughter of John Gardiner; she was born 11 December, 1699.

In 1729, was appointed Coroner; also represented Woodstock in Massachusetts General Court.

When the County of Worcester was formed, and his father was appointed Judge, he was made Clerk of the Courts, and moved with his family to Worcester, the county seat, where he lived the rest of his life. He was Moderator of a town meeting in 1733, and often afterwards. He represented Worcester in the General Court, 1732–42; was Selectman, 1733–35, 1737–40, and 1742–53; Town Treasurer, 1741–52; County Treasurer, 1731–62; Clerk of all the Courts, 1731–52; Sheriff, 1751–62; Register of Probate to 1757, and Register of Deeds, 1731–61.

His wife Hannah died 5 January, 1738–9, aged thirty-nine, and 28 January, 1739–40, he married Mrs. Sarah (Clark) Paine, widow of Hon. Nathaniel Paine.

In 1754, he succeeded his father in the higher office of Judge of the County Courts, and was made Chief Justice in 1757, continuing to preside over them to 1762. He was also Judge of

Probate from 1756 to his death in 1762, Colonel of the Militia, and a member of his Majesty's Council.

In 1754, he was one of the delegates appointed by Governor Shirley to treat with the Five Nations, and concert measures for a union of the British-American Colonies, the germ of the American Union. He lived on a liberal scale, was jovial in temper, and fond of hospitality. "His talents," says Lincoln, "were brilliant and showy, rather than solid and profound."

He gave the church in Worcester a communion service and a folio Bible, and contributed freely towards a new building. He lived on the Earl Place, east of Summer Street, in Worcester, and died 10 or 12 August, 1762, wealthy and full of honors.

His widow Sarah died 13 August, 1778. Their portraits by Smibert are in existence.

Children — all by first wife.

1. Mary, born in New London, 9 September 1717.
2. Esther, born in New London, 23 May, 1719.
3. JOHN, born in New London, 26 February, 1720–1.
4. Gardiner, born in Woodstock, 18 September, 1723.
5. Sarah, born in Woodstock, 11 January, 1725–6.
6. Hannah, born in Woodstock, 1 February, 1727–8.
7. Lucretia, born 18 July, 1730.
8. Elizabeth, born 5 January, 1732–3.
9. Katharine, born 28 March, 1735.

Hon. JOHN CHANDLER (4th), of Worcester; commonly known as "Tory John," or as the "Honest Refugee." Born in New London, 26 February, 1720–1.

When Worcester County was formed in 1731, and his grandfather became Judge of the County Courts, his father was appointed Clerk, and moved with his family to Worcester.

John Chandler (4th), married 4 or 5 March, 1740–1, Dorothy, daughter of Col. Nathaniel Paine, of Bristol, R. I. She was born 20 January, 1723–4, and died in Worcester, 5 October, 1745.

He married second wife, 11 June, 1746, Mary, daughter of

Col. Charles Church, of Bristol, R. I. She was born between 1721 and 1725.

Chandler held the following offices: Selectman, 1748–59, 1761–73; Town Treasurer, 1753–60; Town Clerk, 1764–68; Representative, 1752–55; County Treasurer, 1762–74; Sheriff of Worcester County, 1754–62; Judge of Probate, 1762–74.

In 1757, he marched as Colonel at the head of his regiment to the relief of Fort William Henry.

Up to 1774, his life had been an almost unbroken career of prosperity, but his chivalrous sense of loyalty brought him into direct conflict with the rising flood of Revolutionary sentiment, and he was exiled with five other prominent loyalists of Worcester. Leaving his home and family in 1774, he retired to Boston, and thence, in 1776, to Halifax, and finally to London, where he died 26 September, 1800, and was buried at Islington. On his departure from Worcester his estate was probated; part was set off to his wife as her dower, and the rest was confiscated; the total of the estate being stated by the British Commissioners at over £36,000. Chandler never returned to America. His wife died at Worcester, 11 September, 1783.

An original portrait of Chandler hangs in the American Antiquarian Society's building.

Children — by first wife, Dorothy:

1. John, born 3 March, 1741–2.
2. Gardiner, died young.
3. Clark, born 1 December, 1743.
4. Dorothy, born 16 September, 1745.

By second wife, Mary:

5. Rufus, born 18 May, 1747. H. C. 1766.
6. Gardiner, born 27 January, 1749.
7. Nathaniel, born 6 November, 1750. H. C. 1768.
8. William, born 7 December, 1752. H. C. 1772.
9. Charles, born 22 January, 1755.
10. Samuel, born 25 February, 1757.
11. Sarah, born 14 December, 1758.
12. Mary, born 21 December, 1759.

13. Benjamin, born 15 August, 1761; died young.
14. Francis, born 28 July, 1763; died young.
15. LUCRETIA, born 9 June, 1765. Married Aaron Bancroft.
16. Thomas, born 11 January, 1768. H. C. 1787.
17. Elizabeth, born 20 February, 1770.

DOUGLAS.

William.
Elizabeth, married John Chandler (1st).

WILLIAM DOUGLAS, of Boston. 1640 immigrant. Born about 1610 in England. Came over, with his wife Ann and two children; moved, 1641, to Ipswich; 1645, to Boston again; freeman, 1646; a cooper by trade; bought and sold land in Boston 1646–1648.

In 1659, bought house and land in New London, and in 1660 moved there with wife and three children, two daughters being already married. In New London he became a leading citizen; was chosen "townsman" 1663, 1666, 1667; Recorder and Moderator, 1667, 1668; sealer and packer, 1673, 1674; Deputy to General Court, 1672 and after; Deacon from 1670 to his death, which took place 26 July, 1682, in the 72d year of his age.

Wife, Anne, born about 1610, was daughter of Thomas Mattle, of Ringstead, Northamptonshire, England. About 1670 she laid claim by inheritance to property in Ringstead. She died about 1685.
Children:

1. Ann, born in England, 1637.
2. Robert, born in England, 1639.
3. ELIZABETH, born in Ipswich, Mass. 26 August, 1641; married Deacon John Chandler (1st).
4. Sarah, born in Ipswich, 8 April, 1643.
5. William, born in Boston, 1 April, 1645.

Much fuller details may be found in the Douglas Genealogy, Providence, 1879.

RAYMOND.

Richard.
Joshua.
Mary, married John Chandler (2d).

RICHARD RAYMOND, of Salem. Immigrant. Wife Judith. Freeman, 14 May, 1634; removed from Massachusetts by 1658; was in Norwalk, Conn., 1664; removed 1664 to Saybrook. Died there, 1692.

Children:

1. Bathsheba, baptized 11 July, 1637.
2. JOSHUA, baptized 3 March, 1639.
3. Lemuel, baptized 3 January, 1641.
4. Hannah, baptized February, 1643.
5. Samuel, baptized 13 July, 1645.
6. Richard, baptized 2 January, 1648.
7. Elizabeth, baptized 28 April, 1650.
8. Daniel, baptized 17 April, 1653.

———

JOSHUA RAYMOND, New London, 1658; son of Richard. Baptized 3 March, 1639.

Married, 10 December, 1659, Elizabeth, daughter of Nehemiah Smith.

Raymond died 1676.

Widow Elizabeth, in 1676, appointed administratrix of estate in Block Island.

She married, 26 January, 1681, George Dennis.

Children:

1. Joshua, born 18 September, 1660.
2. Elizabeth, born 24 May, 1662.
3. Ann, born 12 May, 1664.
4. Hannah, born 8 August, 1668.
5. MARY, born 12 March, 1671-2; married John Chandler (2d).
6. Experience, born 20 January, 1674.

SMITH.

Nehemiah.
Elizabeth, married Joshua Raymond.

NEHEMIAH SMITH, of New Haven. Immigrant. Wife Sarah ———.

Kept the sheep of the town 1644–9; removed soon after to New London, and thence, about 1660, to Norwich.

Freeman, 1669; died 1686, leaving widow Ann (presumably his second wife) and four daughters.

Children — by wife, Sarah:

1. Sarah, born 1642, baptized 14 December, 1645.
2. Mary, born 1642, baptized 14 December, 1645.
3. Hannah, born 1644, baptized 14 December, 1645.
4. Mercy, born 1645, baptized 22 February, 1646.
5. ELIZABETH, born 1645, baptized 22 February, 1646; married Joshua Raymond.
6. Nehemiah, born 1646.

(List of children taken from "Baptisms" in New Haven, Conn., N. E. H. G. Reg. IX, 362. Cf. XIV, 82.)

GARDINER.

Lion.
David.
John.
Hannah, married John Chandler (3d).

LION GARDINER is a well-defined character, the most picturesque figure among our sketches. His life is well-known, for we have extant many of his letters, an autobiographic narrative of his share in the Indian wars, and other original documents relating to his life. Singularly enough, he throws no light on his birth, family, or early years.

He was an English Puritan, born about 1599; on reaching manhood he entered the service of the Prince of Orange as military engineer. While thus employed, he met persons interested with Lord Say, Lord Brook, and others in the New England emigration, and at the persuasion of Hugh Peters entered into a contract to serve them in America for four years at £100 a year as a military engineer.

About this time, he married Mary, daughter of Dericke Wilemson and Hochim Bastians, of Woerden, Holland, (born 1601), and on 10 July, 1635, with his wife, a maid-servant, and a "work-master," he left Woerden, sailed from Rotterdam to London in the "Bacheler", a vessel of twenty-five tons, and thence, 16 August, 1635, to Boston, where they arrived 28 November. While delayed there, he was employed on the defenses of Fort Hill; but in the spring of 1636, they continued their voyage in the "Bacheler" to the mouth of Connecticut River.

There he erected Saybrook Fort in the face of great difficulties, and maintained it against the attacks of hostile Indians till the end of his contract in 1639, of which experience he has left a written account. Two children were born to him in the fort.

In May, 1639, he purchased of friendly Indians an island lying just east of Long Island, now known as Gardiner's Island, whither he soon moved with his family, taking along some of his men, and making it his home till 1653. It was a bold move, but he relied for defense on the friendship of the Montauk Indians, with whom he maintained relations of mutual good service.

In 1653, he moved to East Hampton, L. I., where he died, in 1663, aged sixty-four, leaving a considerable estate. His will was dated 13 August, 1658, and the inventories filed April, 1664. His widow, Mary, died 1665, aged sixty-four.

Although settled in what is now New York, his relations were all with New England. He was a man of bold, positive character, and much respected by his contemporaries.

Children:

1. DAVID, born 29 April, 1636.
2. Mary, born 30 August, 1638.
3. Elizabeth, born 14 September, 1641.

DAVID GARDINER, of Gardiner's Island; son of Lion. Born 29 April, 1636, in Saybrook Fort.

About 1656, visited England, and there married, 4 June, 1657, Mrs. Mary Leringman, widow. He is found again in Southold, Long Island, 10 June, 1658.

Nothing more is known of wife Mary; she is not mentioned in Lion Gardiner's will nor in his widow's. Apparently the connection was displeasing to the family. Lion Gardiner's widow died in 1665, and left to David the manor of Gardiner's Island. He also owned land in Southold, where, perhaps, he removed later.

He died, 10 July, 1689, in his 54th year, at Hartford, while in attendance upon the General Assembly of Connecticut, and was buried there; he left no will.

Children:

1. JOHN, born 19 April, 1661.
2. David.
3. Elizabeth.
4. Lion.

JOHN GARDINER, of Gardiner's Island; son of David. Born 19 April, 1661.

Married, first, Mary, daughter of Samuel King, of Southold. She died 4 July, 1707, aged 37, and was buried at East Hampton; seven children.

Gardiner married, second, 2 September, 1708, Mrs. Sarah (Chandler) Coit, widow; she died 3 July, 1711, and was buried at East Hampton; two children.

He married, third, 13 July, 1713, Elizabeth, daughter of John Allyn; she died and was buried on Gardiner's Island; no children.

Gardiner married, fourth, 4 October, 1733, Mrs. Elizabeth (Hedges) Osborne, widow; no children. She died 19 May, 1747, aged 64, and was buried at East Hampton.

Gardiner's name appears on several real estate transactions in Southold.

In 1699, the notorious Captain Kidd remained some time off Gardiner's Island, and left in Gardiner's charge considerable merchandise and treasure; the latter amounting to 1,111 ozs. gold and 2,353 ozs. silver, besides some jewels. Gardiner was ignorant of the character of his visitor, and when Kidd was arrested he surrendered the property to the Governor of Massachusetts Bay. He died, 25 June, 1738, of injuries received, by a fall from a horse at Groton, and was buried at New London.

John Gardiner's will, made 14 December, 1737, and proved 1 August, 1738, gives "my well-beloved daughter, Hannah Chandler, the sum of 150 pounds in silver money at eight shillings the ounce Troy weight"; also, gives "my grand-daughter, Sarah Chandler, fifty pounds in New England money"; also makes Hannah Chandler one of the residuary legatees.

An old record says, "John was a hearty, active, robust man, generous and upright, sober at home, but jovial abroad; and swore sometimes."

Children — by first wife:

1. David, born 3 January, 1691.
2. John, born 1693.   Yale 1711.
3. Samuel, born 1695.
4. Joseph, born 22 April, 1697.
5. HANNAH, born 11 December, 1699; married John Chandler (3d).
6. Mary, born 1 September, 1702.
7. Elizabeth.

By second wife:

8. Jonathan, born 1709.
9. Sarah, born 1710.

For fuller details of the Gardiner family see "Lion Gardiner, and His Descendants," by C. C. Gardiner, St. Louis, 1890.

KING.

William.
Samuel.
Mary, married John Gardiner.

WILLIAM KING, of Salem. Immigrant. Born in England about 1595.

Sailed in the "Abigail," from Weymouth, Dorsetshire, March 1635–6, aged forty, with wife Dorothy, aged thirty-four, and five children—Mary, 12 years; Katheryn, 10; William, 8; Hannah, 6, and Samuel, 2.

The register of the Abbey Church of St. Mary in Sherburne, Dorsetshire, contains this record, "1616–7, Feb. 17, Williami Kinge et Dorothiae Hayne nupt."

William King settled at Salem; freeman, 25 May, 1636; received grants of land; homestead at Beverly; grand juror, 1637; member First Church, Salem, but his wife's name is not on the rolls. He was an Antinomian, and in 1637, says Savage, was one of five men in Salem required to be disarmed for the public safety.

He died 1650–1, intestate; the settlement of his estate shows three sons, four daughters, two married and two unmarried.

Widow Dorothy, in 1652, bought land of John Swazey, husband of her daughter Katheryn, which she sold in 1653. In 1658, she is mentioned as the "widow and relict of William King, Senior."

Another document states that she sold her homestead to her son William, and removed to Long Island, N. Y., where she was living in 1684. She probably died at Southold, L. I., where two of her married daughters and her son Samuel were living.

Children:

1. Mary, born in England; married Scudder.
2. Katheryn, born in England; married John Swazey.
3. William, born in England; eldest son.
4. Hannah, born in England; married Richard Browne, Sr.
5. SAMUEL, born in England about 1633.
6. Mehitable, born in America, 25 December, 1636.

7. John, born in America, 1 November, 1638.
8. Deliverance, born in America, 31 October, 1641.

SAMUEL KING, of Southold, L. I.; son of William. Born in England about 1633.

Came to America 1635–6 with his father, William, who lived in Salem. After his father's death, in 1650–1, his mother removed to Southold, L. I., probably taking her younger children with her.

Samuel King is recorded in 1658 as owning 400 acres in Southold. He married, before 1670, Abigail, daughter of William Ludlam, Sr.

In 1710, King gave a deed of land in Salem to his son John. He died 29 November, 1721, aged 88.

Children:

1. John.
2. MARY, born 1670; married John Gardiner.
    Perhaps other children.

LUDLAM.

WILLIAM LUDLAM, of Southampton, L. I. Immigrant. Was formerly of Matlock in Derbyshire, England, where he was entitled to a considerable estate, which his grandson, William Ludlam, Jr., in 1710, appointed Thomas Cardale, Gent., his attorney, to collect.

Wife Clemence.

Children:

ABIGAIL, married Samuel King.
    And probably other children.

CHURCH.

Richard.
Benjamin.
Charles.
Mary, married John Chandler (4th).

RICHARD CHURCH, of Duxbury. Immigrant. Born 1608.

Came to America in 1630, in the fleet with Governor Winthrop; made freeman 19 October, 1630, but did not take the oath; moved from Weymouth to Plymouth 1631.

He having left the Bay without permission, the Bay authorities remonstrated with the Plymouth Government because they harbored him. The Governor and Council replied: "Richard Church came as a sojourner to work for the present, though he is still here resident longer than he purposed; and what he will do neither we nor I think himself knows, but if he resolve to settle here we shall require of him to procure a dismissal. But he did affirm to us at the first that he was one of Mr. Webb's men and freed to go to England or whither he would,— the which we rather believed because he came to us from Wessagussett upon the falling out with his partner."

Church was made freeman of Plymouth Colony, 4 October, 1632. March, 1633, gave deed to Robert Bartlett.

In 1636, married Elizabeth, daughter of Richard Warren; lived at Eel River, Plymouth.

In 1637, taxed at Duxbury; a carpenter by trade; same year built first meeting-house at Plymouth; in 1647, exchanged lands at Eel River with Manasseh Kempton; in 1649, sold estate at Eel River for £25 to Robert Bartlett, taking in part payment a red ox, valued at £8–10; was at Eastham in 1649; at Charlestown in 1653; at Hingham in 1657, where he made his final residence; made will at Hingham, 25 December, 1668, signing with his ": mark," and died at Dedham, 27 December, 1668.

He served as Sergeant in the Pequot War; was often a member of the "Grand Enquest" and was frequently made referee.

His widow died at Hingham, 4 March, 1670.

Children:

1. Elizabeth.
2. Joseph, born 1638.
3. BENJAMIN, born 1639; married Alice Southworth.
4. Nathaniel, born 1642.
5. Caleb.
6. Charles.
7. Richard.
8. Abigail, born 1648.
9. Hannah.
10. Sarah.
11. Lydia.
12. Priscilla.
13. Deborah, born 1657.

Colonel BENJAMIN CHURCH, of Bristol and Little Compton, the famous Indian fighter; son of Richard. Born in 1639, at Plymouth. Bred to his father's trade, a carpenter; in 1667, was living at Little Compton.

On 26 December, 1667, married Alice, daughter of Constant Southworth, of Duxbury. She was born about 1646.

On 29 May, 1670, freeman at Duxbury; June, 1671, Constable there.

The breaking out of King Philip's War in 1675 gave scope for his military ability, and made him a historic character. He joined the little army in December, 1675, as aid upon the staff of Governor Winslow, the Commander-in-Chief, and took a leading part in the actual field-service of the war. He was in command of the final expedition resulting in the death of King Philip, 12 August, 1676.

In 1692, he again enlisted in the service against the Indians; and in 1696 he raised a force for the defense of Maine, returning with valuable captures, cannon, stores, etc.

Again, in 1704, though sixty-five years old, he conducted a vigorous campaign against the Maine hostiles, with a force of 1200 men.

Later in life, he embodied his recollections of King Philip's War in a book (1716), which is one of the chief authorities on the war.

On 14 September, 1680, he signed the articles for the settlement of Bristol; the next year he was authorized by the General Court to clear a road from Mount Hope to Boston, and in September, 1681, he headed the list of proprietors changing the name from Mount Hope to Bristol.

On 22 May, 1682, chosen Deputy to represent Bristol in the General Court; at the same time chosen First Selectman; both of which positions he held during his residence in Bristol. On 7 July, 1682, commissioned as a magistrate.

In 1687, one of the original eight members of First Congregational Church of Bristol.

He refused a military commission under Governor Andros, but, in 1689-90, he took command of the expedition against the Indians of Maine.

Probably in 1696, or '97, he moved to Freetown (now Fall River) and built mills, which he sold in 1714.

In 1705, he moved to Little Compton, where he was chosen Representative in 1706. He often acted as Moderator there in town meetings, and served as trial justice.

On 16 January, 1717-18, he was thrown from a horse, and died the next day, in the 78th year of his age.

His widow Alice died at Little Compton, 5 March, 1719, aged 73.

Children:

1. Thomas, born at Duxbury, 1673 or '74.
2. Constant, born at Portsmouth, R. I., 12 May, 1676.
3. Benjamin, born 1678.
4. Edward, born 1680.
5. CHARLES, born 9 May, 1682.
6. Elizabeth, born 26 March, 1684.
7. Nathaniel, born 1 July, 1686.
8. Martha.

Colonel CHARLES CHURCH, of Bristol; son of Colonel Benjamin. Born 9 May, 1682.

Married 20 May, 1708, Hannah, daughter Hon. Nathaniel Paine. She was born 20 April, 1685. They lived in Bristol.

In 1712, he was on committee to take down belfry; in 1722, joined Bristol Church with wife Hannah; in 1730, with brother Thomas, petitioned General Court for land, as recompense for father's services; 500 acres were granted to family of Benjamin Church.

He was often on the town committees and held various offices; was Sheriff, Field Driver, Assessor, Representative.

He died January, 1747, aged 65, at Bristol; will made 29 November, 1746, proved 24 February, 1747; inventory, £1153. 3s. 6d.; among other property, six negroes; Church's death is noticed in the News Letter of 8 January, 1747.

His widow Hannah died 16 October, 1755, aged 70.

Her will made 28 May, 1755; proved 19 November, 1755; inventory £2439. 8s. 4d. Both wills contain legacies to their daughter Mary Chandler.

Church was one of the subscribers to Prince's History.

Children:

1. Constant, born 12 December, 1708; baptized at Bristol, 5 August, 1721.
2. Elizabeth, born 24 December, 1710; baptized at Bristol, 5 August, 1721.
3. Hannah, born 20 February, 1713; baptized at Bristol, 5 August, 1721.
4. Nathaniel, baptized at Bristol, 5 August, 1721.
5. Dorothy, baptized at Bristol, 5 August, 1721.
6. Sarah, baptized at Bristol, 5 August, 1721.
7. MARY, married John Chandler (4th).

WARREN.

Richard.
Elizabeth, married Richard Church.

RICHARD WARREN, Plymouth, 1620. Immigrant. Came in the "Mayflower," leaving family in England.

He was a brother of Robert, parson of Rame, Cornwall, and of John, of Boston; was a London merchant; did not go to Leyden; joined the "Mayflower" at Plymouth; married, in England, Mrs. Elizabeth Marsh (maiden name, Carpenter), widow; seven children, all born in England. She followed Warren, in 1623, with five daughters; the two sons also came to America before 1627, exact date unknown, probably 1621.

Warren signed "the Compact," 11 November, 1620, on board the "Mayflower" off Provincetown, being twelfth in order out of forty-one. In the roll of the "Mayflower" passengers, he has the prefix "Mr."; he was one of the exploring party which left the "Mayflower," 16 December, in the shallop, and discovered Plymouth Harbor; returning to the ship, 23 December. "He is mentioned by Bradford as a most useful man during the short time he lived."

In 1623, at the partition of lands, his lot was assigned him near Eel River, and the farm remained in his family over 200 years.

In the division of cattle, in 1627, the ninth lot fell to Richard Warren and his company, consisting of himself, wife, two sons, and five daughters, and four others; to them fell one of the four black heifers that came in the "Jacob," called the smooth-faced heifer.

Warren died in 1628, aged about forty-five or fifty. "He was a useful instrument, and during his life bore a deep share in the difficulties and troubles of the first settlement."

His widow survived him forty-five years; her name is found on the tax-list of 1632–3, her rates being £0. 12s. 0d.; and she is mentioned in the will of her son Nathaniel, 29 November, 1667. She died 2 October, 1673, aged about ninety-two. "Having lived a godly life, she came to her grave as a shock fully ripe."

Children — all born in England:

1. Mary; married in 1628, Robert Bartlett.
2. Ann; married, 19 April, 1633, Thomas Little.
3. Sarah; married, 28 March, 1634, John Cooke.
4. ELIZABETH; married in 1636, Richard Church.
5. Abigail; married in 1639, Anthony Snow.
6. Nathaniel; married in 1645, Mary (or Sarah) Walker.
7. Joseph; married about 1651, Priscilla Faunce.

SOUTHWORTH.

CONSTANT SOUTHWORTH, of Duxbury. Immigrant. Born in Leyden, Holland, 1614.

His father, Edward Southworth, was early at Leyden, where he married, 28 May, 1613, Alice, daughter of Alexander Carpenter, who came to Leyden before 1612, from Wrington, near Bath, England.

Edward Southworth died at Leyden in 1621, and his widow came over to Plymouth, Mass., in the "Ann," in 1623, aged thirty-three, and married Governor William Bradford, 14 August, 1623.

Constant followed his mother in 1628, being fourteen years old. He paid for his trip — "for passage, £1; eleven weeks' diet, at 4s. 6d., £2. 11s. 4d.; total, £3. 11s. 4d."

Governor Bradford superintended his education; he was made freeman of the Colony, married Elizabeth, daughter of William Collier, of Duxbury, 2 November, 1637, and settled at Duxbury; the same year he volunteered for service in the Pequot War. In 1643, his name is among "those able to bear arms" at Duxbury.

His upright character is testified by the important trusts reposed in him, and by the style of men associated with him.

On 29 October, 1652, James Lindall made him "supervisor" of his will, the witnesses being John Alden and Miles Standish; and the Court appointed him guardian of Lindall's children; in

1662, with Alden, he witnessed will of Edmond Chandler, and in 1663, he and Alden inventoried estate of Zachariah Soule; in 1669, his brother Thomas made him a bequest, charging him with "the support of my wife in her poor condition."

His strong connections by marriage with Governor Bradford and William Collier, two of the most influential men in the Colony, brought him early into public notice, and he was made Deputy from Duxbury in 1647, in which capacity he served for seventeen years, and in 1670, on the death of his brother Thomas, he succeeded him as an Assistant; in 1663, he became Treasurer of the Colony, filling both these positions up to his death in 1679. He also served once as Commissioner for Plymouth in the Congress of the United Colonies; in April, 1671, he was sent as one of a special commission from Plymouth to a meeting of the representatives of the English Colonies with Philip, at Taunton, to arrange terms of peace. Later the same year, he took, with others, a letter from Plymouth to the Government of Rhode Island on the same subject.

His mother, Mrs. Bradford, died 26 March, 1670–1, aged about eighty, leaving him a legacy in her will, which she signed with her "mark." The Colonial records speak of her as a "godly matron, much loved while she lived, and lamented when she died."

In 1661, Southworth was instructed by the Court to attend the meetings of the Quakers, then frequent in Duxbury, and refute the errors set forth. At one time he was appointed to sell beer and liquors, such traffic being then limited to the hands of responsible citizens.

Some of his transactions in land and otherwise have survived upon the records: In 1660, in division of lands at Freetown (Fall River), he received the nineteenth lot; in 1667, Philip sold to Southworth and others for £15 all the meadow lands from Dartmouth to Mattapoisett; in 1672, Philip conveyed to Southworth, apparently in trust, for £47, a large tract of land near Taunton, which he assigned to the inhabitants of Taunton; in 1675, Watuspaquin and others conveyed to Southworth and others "all that tract of land known as 'Assowamsett,' " etc.; and in 1677, with three others, he hired "the fishing privileges and profits at the Cape," for seven years, at £30 per year; in 1675, he was ordered, with William Paybody, to run the line between Bridgewater and Middleboro.

In 1675, though sixty-one years old, he joined the army on the breaking out of King Philip's War, as Commissary General, but soon yielded the place to his son-in-law, Colonel Benjamin Church.

Southworth died, 11 March, 1679. His will cut off his daughter Elizabeth with five shillings, if she married William Fobes, which, I am glad to say, she did.

Mrs. Southworth is said to have died 26 March, 1670; but perhaps she was mistaken for Mrs. Bradford, who died about that time.

Children:

1. Edward.
2. Nathaniel, born 1648.
3. William, born 1659.
4. Mercy.
5. ALICE, married Benjamin Church.
6. Mary.
7. Elizabeth.
8. Priscilla.

_____

COLLIER.

WILLIAM COLLIER, of Duxbury. Immigrant. A merchant of London; one of the "adventurers"; came over before 1632, with four daughters.

In 1632, petitioned General Court for incorporation of Duxbury as a town; in January, 1633-4, on Board of Assessors for Colony, his own tax-rate being £2. 5s. 0d.; Edward Winslow and he paid the heaviest rate in the Colony. Collier was not only a man of substance, but also of great influence and position.

In 1634, he was made Assistant, serving in that capacity for twenty-eight years, in the period from 1634 to 1665; in 1643, he was one of the two Commissioners sent from Plymouth to the

Congress of the United Colonies; in 1657, he presided over the General Court "for two periods."

His name is often found on the records in the settlement of the estates of his friends. In company with Miles Standish, he inventoried the estate of William King in 1641; that of Love Brewster in 1650; and of James Lyndall in 1652; William Thomas made him his executor in 1651, leaving him a "silver beer-bowl"; in 1658, with John Alden and Constant Southworth, he inventoried estate of Rev. Ralph Partridge.

In 1652, among first purchasers of Dartmouth; in 1660, licensed to sell beer, wine, etc., although he was the wealthiest man in the Colony; it being the custom at Plymouth to put this traffic in the hands of the most responsible citizens; in 1662, conference at his house in Duxbury between Sachem Alexander and several magistrates.

Collier was rigid, narrow, and illiberal in his views; with three others, he tried and convicted Howland for harboring a Quaker preacher and resisting an officer who tried to arrest the preacher; at another time he declared he would not remain in the General Court, if Cudworth, the Quakers' friend were admitted. He died in 1670.

Children— all born in England:

1. Sarah; married in 1634, Love Brewster.
2. Rebecca; married in 1634, Job Cole.
3. Mary; married (second wife), in 1635, Thomas Prence.
4. ELIZABETH; married, 2 November, 1637, Constant Southworth.

PAINE.

Stephen.
Nathaniel.
Nathaniel.
Hannah, married Charles Church.

STEPHEN PAINE, of Rehoboth. Immigrant. He was a miller in England; came from Great Ellingham, near Hingham, Norfolk County, England, in 1638, with wife, Rose, three sons, and four servants, by ship "Diligent," of Ipswich; land granted him at Hingham, Mass., and he settled there. Freeman, 6 June, 1639; Representative, 1641.

In 1641, had land granted him in Seekonk; asked leave to move there, which he did in 1643-4; name of town changed to Rehoboth. He became prominent in the affairs of the new town; his name often appears on the records in offices of honor and trust; he became wealthy; in 1643, his estate was valued at £535; in 1644, he was elected "townsman" for general management of town affairs; which office he held for several years.

In 1645, chosen Deputy to General Court; which office he held to 1660, and various times after that up to 1671.

In 1645, his name appears in a division of town land; also one of committee to lay out land for John Brown.

On 30 March, 1647, inventoried estate of Alex. Winchester, of Rehoboth; on 3 November, 1647, witnessed will of Henry Smith, of Rehoboth; in 1648, bought land of Governor Bradford; on 4 October, 1649, "overseer" of will of Thomas Bliss, of Rehoboth, and inventoried estate.

In 1656, one of three appointed to determine controversies, value not over £3; in 1661, with others purchased from Indians large tract of land adjoining Rehoboth; in 1662, inventoried estates of John Brown, Jr., and John Brown, Sr., both of Rehoboth; in 1666, appointed with others by proprietors of Swansey to divide the land.

There are also various other details of minor matters concerning him in the records; he was an extensive land-owner.

Wife Rose died 20 January, 1660-1; he married in 1662, second wife, Widow Alice Parker; she is also called Elizabeth in his will made July, 1679. He died August, 1679, leaving a very large estate.

Widow Alice died 5 December, 1682.

Children — born in England:

1. Stephen, born 1629.
2. NATHANIEL.
   A third son, name unknown, is mentioned.

NATHANIEL PAINE, of Rehoboth; son of Stephen. Born in England. Came to America with his parents in 1638; settled in Rehoboth; merchant, in business with his parents. Wife, Elizabeth ———; parentage unknown.

In 1653, purchased land in Swansey from Indians; in 1667, with four others on a committee to regulate admission to the town of Swansey, and to divide the land.

In 1675, on committee to negotiate with King Philip; in 1675–6, contributed £100 for expenses of Indian War; in 1676–7, Deputy to General Court.

Latter part of his life lived in Boston; and died there, 1678, intestate, leaving a large property.

Widow Elizabeth died in Boston about 1704.

Child:

NATHANIEL, born in Rehoboth, 18 October, 1661.

Hon. NATHANIEL PAINE (2d); son of Nathaniel. Born in Rehoboth, 18 October, 1661.

Married about 1680–1, Dorothy, daughter of Jonathan Rainsford, of Boston. Removed early to Bristol, of which he was an original proprietor; his name appearing on town records in 1681.

Selectman, 1696; same year admitted member of Bristol Church, with wife Dorothy.

In 1710, appointed Judge of Inferior Court of Common Pleas; same year appointed Judge of Probate for Bristol County; retained position of Judge of Probate for five years; retained position of Judge of Court of Common Pleas till his death, in 1723, being Chief Justice the latter part of the time.

One of the Council of Massachusetts Bay from 1703 to his death, in 1723, except one year.

He died at Bristol, 28 February, 1723–4; widow Dorothy died January, 1755.

Children:

1. Elizabeth, born 6 November, 1681.
2. Mary, born 8 June, 1683.

3. HANNAH, born 20 April, 1685; married Charles Church.
4. Nathaniel, born 9 March, 1688. (Ancestor of the Worcester Paines.)
5. Edward, born 7 October, 1690.
6. Jonathan, born 18 April, 1695.
7. Alathea, born 28 August, 1697.
8. Sarah, born 5 May, 1699.
9. Stephen, born 1701; H. C., 1721; Register of Probate; Judge of Court of Common Pleas; Representative to General Court.
10. Dorothy, } twins, born 19 March, 1706-7.
11. Sarah,

Principal source of information concerning the Paines: "The Paine Family," by Nathaniel Paine, of Worcester.

RAINSFORD.
Edward.
Jonathan.
Dorothy, married Nathaniel Paine.

EDWARD RAINSFORD. Immigrant. Boston, 1630; came in the fleet with Winthrop; first wife died June, 1632; two children. In Dorchester town records, 6 January, 1633, "ordered that Moses Maverick shall have the lot that was allotted" to Edward Rainsford.

On 2 June, 1634, records mention "Mr. Rainsford's house in Boston."

He married about 1633, second wife, Elizabeth; nine children, whose births are all on the Boston records; on 17 April, 1637, made freeman.

On 18 May, 1639, the dead body of Peter Fitchew was found "in the salt water, near the house of Mr. Rainsford," in Boston.

On 13 January, 1648-9, mentioned in accounts of estate of Henry Kemball; in 1649, witnessed will of John Gallop; in 1651, mentioned in Jacob Elliot's will; on 16 March, 1653, deposition in estate of Elias Maineyerd; in 1655, overseer of will of Chr.

Gallop; in 1656, inventoried estate of Samuel Johnson; in 1662, inventoried estate of George Pearse; in 1662, overseer of will of William Colbron; in 1663, among debtors to estate of David Evans; in 1663-4, inventoried three estates; in 1668, overseer of will of Thomas Snow.

Savage says he was Deacon and Ruling Elder of the First Church, Boston, and one of the founders of the Third Church; on 16 February, 1669-70, made Ruling Elder of the Third Church.

On 10 March, 1676, "Mr. Ransford" mentioned in Judge Sewall's diary.

Will made 3 August, 1680; died 16 August, 1680.

Widow Elizabeth died 16 November, 1688, aged eighty-one.

Children—by first wife:

1. Mary, born 1 June, 1632.
2. Joshua, or Josiah, born 1 June, 1632; died September, 1632.

By second wife:

3. John, born 30 June, 1634.
4. JONATHAN, born October, 1636.
5. Ranis, born 4 June, 1638.
6. Nathan, born 24 July, 1641.
7. David, baptized 1 September, 1644.
8. Solomon.
9. Edward.
10. Elizabeth.
11. Ann, born 1 February, 1651-2.

JONATHAN RAINSFORD, Boston; son of Edward. Baptized 23 October, 1636; married, 29 November, 1656, by Richard Bellingham, Deputy-Governor, Mary, daughter of John Sunderland.

In 1660, mentioned in accounts of estate of Thomas Thornhill; in 1664, mentioned in proceedings about will of Samuel Maverick, Jr.

Rainsford died at Barbadoes, 11 March, 1671.

Widow Mary married August, 1674, Joshua Hobart.

Children:

1. Mary, born 2 July, 1659.
2. Jonathan, born 26 July, 1661.
3. DOROTHY, born 11 September, 1663; married Nathaniel Paine.
4. Hannah, born 5 April, 1666.

SUNDERLAND.

John.
Mary, married Jonathan Rainsford.

JOHN SUNDERLAND, Boston. Immigrant. Born about 1619. First mention is birth of son John on Boston records, 1640.

Admitted to church, 9 April, 1643.

Freeman, 10 May, 1643; styled himself parchment-maker; wife Dorothy admitted to church, 4 April, 1646; six children.

Between 1651 and 1669, his name appears frequently on the Boston records, mainly in the settlement of estates.

In 1651, he was a creditor of Henry Sanders; in 1652, a debtor to Captain Bozone Allen; in 1654 and 1655, he inventoried two estates; in 1656, mentioned in accounts of Arthur Gill.

In 1658, he was a member of the Artillery Company.

In 1658-62, he inventoried six estates; in 1660, appeared as a creditor in the accounts of Captain Thomas Thornhill; in 1663, among debtors reckoned good, of David Evans.

On 29 January, 1664, wife Dorothy died; and he married (date unknown), second wife, Thomasine, daughter of William Lumpkin, and widow of Samuel Mayo.

In 1664 and 1665, inventoried two estates; in 1669, "overseer" with Godfrey Armitage, of will of Elizabeth Bitfield, who gave him 50s., "as a token of my love."

In 1672, made conveyance of his goods to John Vial, in trust for daughter-in-law Mary, and her children; she was the daughter of Vial.

He seems to have been unfortunate in his later years; he lost his property and removed to Eastham, where he died 26 December, 1703, in his eighty-fifth year.

Widow Thomasine died at Eastham, 16 June, 1709, in her eighty-fourth year.

Sunderland's will was dated 27 September, 1700, and probated 4 April, 1704.

Children — by first wife, Dorothy.

1. John, born December 1640, at Boston.
2. MARY, born 12 March, 1641-2, at Boston; married Jonathan Rainsford.
3. Hannah, born 29 September, 1644.
4. James, born 18 March, 1647; died young.
5. James (2d), baptized 6 August, 1648.
6. Benjamin, born 26 July, 1652.

By second wife, Thomasine.

7. Mary (2d) (or, perhaps, Mercy), born 15 July, 1665.
8. Samuel, born 14 April, 1668.

www.ingramcontent.com/pod-product-compliance
Lightning Source LLC
Chambersburg PA
CBHW031438270326
41930CB00007B/762